derek acorah's GHOST tOWNs

derek acorah's
GHOSt tOWNs

HarperElement
An Imprint of HarperCollins*Publishers*
77–85 Fulham Palace Road
Hammersmith, London W6 8JB

The website address is: www.thorsonselement.com

and *HarperElement* are trademarks of
HarperCollins*Publishers* Ltd

First published by HarperElement 2006

10 9 8 7 6 5 4 3 2 1

© Flextech Rights Limited 2006
A Ruggie Media Production for LIVINGtv

Derek Acorah asserts the moral right to be
identified as the author of this work

A catalogue record for this book is
available from the British Library

ISBN-13 978-0-00-722954-3
ISBN-10 0-00-722954-2

Printed and bound in Great Britain by
Clays Ltd, St Ives plc

Contents

Introduction

The enormous black-and-silver Ghost Truck rolled into town. This was the start of a whole new journey for me. Where would it lead? I felt very excited. I was taking my own show on the road, going out to meet people the length and breadth of the country and using my mediumship to investigate their Ghost Towns…

Getting the show on the road

How did it all start? Since 2001 I had been working on the highly successful *Most Haunted* television show, but after five series and over 100 investigations I felt it was time to move on. I was asked to stay for one more series and when that was over I was ready for something different. When LIVINGtv offered me the chance to host my own show in a new format, I was delighted.

Richard Woolfe, then director of television for LIVINGtv, and Paul Flexton, managing director of Ruggie Media, who had worked with me on LIVINGtv's *Loose Lips* and *I'm Famous and Frightened*, had a great idea: putting a show on the road – literally. We would go out to the public and investigate their stories. That meant we would investigate shops, offices, pubs, hotels, houses – anywhere in fact where paranormal activity had been reported. Anything could happen – and probably would. I was only too happy to take part.

> **'Derek loved the idea. He was ready for a new challenge. He was really excited about the show and he's loved it ever since. And we're delighted to be working with the best medium in the country.'**
>
> Paul Flexton, executive producer

The show was commissioned in the middle of June 2005 and we had to get moving, as the first series was to go out in October.

The Ghost Towns family

Joining me on my journeys around the country would be Danniella Westbrook and Angus Purden. I first met Danniella on Granada Breeze's *Psychic Livetime*, though I knew of her work as an actress and, later, as a programme presenter. She had been intrigued by the paranormal ever since she had seen a ghost in her own home and had described presenting a programme on the paranormal as her 'dream job', so when the show was put together her name was top of the list.

Strangely enough, Angus also worked as a presenter, was interested in the paranormal and had seen a ghost. As a child he had lived in a house on a hill surrounded by trees, and once he had looked out of his bedroom window and seen a ghostly shape silhouetted there. Later on he had felt guided by his deceased grandmother and had had an accurate psychic reading, but he still didn't accept everything uncritically.

'I have always been fascinated by everything from *déjà vu* to reincarnation, but I've always had a certain amount of scepticism too – a healthy scepticism, if you like! I've always had to analyse and question everything.'

Angus

When I met him we got on very well and I knew that his open-minded approach would be an asset to the show. And in spite of a few scares along the way, he is loving it!

'A mad, crazy job that involved working through the night – I had to do it. And it is great fun!'

Angus

Angus and Danniella had never met before, but they also hit it off straightaway and now they enjoy spending time together talking, drinking coffee and going shopping. I have heard a rumour that Danniella has bought clothes in every town so far. She and Angus have even started shopping for colour-coordinated outfits for the show. As we're usually filming with night-vision cameras, unfortunately the viewing public don't often get the full benefit!

> **'Danniella and I investigate ghosts by night and shops by day. To be honest, I was hoping that I'd be her pet poodle and she'd buy me lots of clothes, but it hasn't worked out that way!'**
>
> Angus

We also work with a very professional and enthusiastic crew. Normally in the fast-paced television world people move on fairly rapidly, but we have the same great team working with us now as at the very beginning, and that's evidence of the camaraderie that has built up on the show.

My tour manager, Ray, is always with us too, and helps everyone out in so many ways – thank you again, Ray!

In fact we all get on so well that I refer to us as 'the *Ghost Towns* family'.

How does it work?

We could go anywhere of course, but so far the towns have been chosen in a number of ways. For the first series it was very much up to the producers where they chose to film. They wanted a variety of settings, not just historic towns but also more modern ones. The only requirements were that there had to be enough people to tell their stories and enough room to get the Ghost Truck in! (This did prove something of a problem in Bedford.) Later on, people started contacting the television company to put forward their own towns. Now we have quite a long list of places to go to…

> **'We don't make any claims. It's for people to make up their own minds. But we've had a huge positive response to the show and a lot of people would just love it to come to their town.'**
>
> Paul

The Ghost Truck spends two days in each town. On the day before we start filming we arrive at a hotel. It may be in the town we are filming in, but it may not. I have no idea where the investigation itself is to take place and the team takes great care not to tell me anything about it in advance. The next morning the Ghost Truck rolls into town and collects people's stories, but I don't go there until the evening, and it's not until I get in the 'Ghost Car' and am driven to the venue that I find out what sort of place we are investigating.

> **'It's not difficult to keep details of the investigation away from Derek. Some people think he's told everything in advance, but there's no way that could happen – or that he could remember it, as he has the most appalling memory. It even takes a while before he can remember the names of the people he's working with! Until he arrives at the location he has no idea where he's going at all.'**
>
> Paul

During the day, as people are relating their stories at the Ghost Truck, our researchers are busy checking them out as far as possible. Angus, Danniella and I do have some opportunity to explore the local area (or go shopping), but the crew are busy meeting local people, hearing their ghost sotries, conducting research and preparing for the shoot.

> **'With hauntings at a private home, we're not able to run independent checks, but we do try to find out more about more public places, just to make sure that we're not going off on a wild goose chase or that people aren't just seeking publicity. As well as ensuring that the**

reports are genuine, we try to follow up those sightings where there may be a real story to uncover – as with Hayley Murton's house in Northampton, for example. And if there have been several reports of paranormal activity at a site, particularly over a period of time, it's definitely going to be well worth further investigation!'

Natalie Ralston, series producer

We film at night for several reasons – in some cases that's when spirits have made themselves known, often to people who are closing up shops and other premises, and of course an investigation would be impossible in pubs, bus stations, shopping centres and other busy areas when they were open to the public. Spirit communication may come in the form of a gentle breeze or a slight tapping, so we also need to eliminate as much outside interference as we can. This isn't always possible – in the case of a pub on a busy main road, for example – but we do our best. During an investigation, if one of the crew inadvertently makes a noise they always let me know as quickly as possible. Sometimes it's difficult to avoid banging into something when you are in a strange place in the dark, or seven or eight people are all crammed together in a toilet!

Although I don't know anything about the location in advance, Angus and Danniella are briefed on the background of the site and the paranormal activity that has been reported there. This is so they can help things along during the course of the investigation if the person who has called us in forgets something that might be relevant or even freezes on camera or under the stress of the investigation. Both Angus and Danniella are experienced presenters and I am always grateful for their help.

The notes they are given also help them to work out who is going on which investigation, though in most cases it is the series producer who makes the decision. If either Angus or Danniella is intrigued by a particular location, however, they can choose to go there. Danniella always accompanies me on the doorstep divinations. Angus just loves the idea of objects moving or lights going on or off, so he checks out those cases whenever possible.

At the end of the day we all go back to the hotel and are usually so tired that we just have a hot drink before going to bed. It's always nice to relax after all the excitement…

What exactly happens in the Ghost Truck?

'The show's become a juggernaut – literally, in fact, in the case of the Ghost Truck.'

Paul

Basically, the Ghost Truck is a big empty oblong truck. As well as being home to the team gathering people's stories, it also has an area where people can talk to camera, a 'History Corner' for the local historian helping us with our investigations, and a seating area where Angus and Danniella can work on their notes or have a cup of coffee.

The truck is very distinctive – and large – and hundreds of people have visited it, sometimes even in one day! Some have stories to tell, others just want to find out what's happening, meet us and maybe discover a little bit more about their town. One thing's for certain – it gets people talking…

The Ghost Truck in Northampton – our first port of call

Doorstep divination

> 'The doorstep divination is my favourite part of the show.
> As a producer, I'm very proud of it, as it's taking Derek to
> the people in a way that's never been done before.'

Paul

How strange it must be to open the door one night and find
a medium and a camera crew on your doorstep. I would be
surprised if it happened to me! But if I feel a psychic pull
towards a house, I know that there is a message from spirit
for someone there and that we should try to deliver it if we
can.

We do try to be respectful. We never knock after ten
o'clock and usually it's before nine. I know that people,
particularly the elderly, may not be keen on letting strangers
into their home, and that's fine. It's up to them. The
message is there, but if they don't wish to receive it at that
time, that's their choice and I respect that. A person did
once refuse on religious grounds, but most people do agree
and get something of value from the reading.

> 'We do make sure before the reading that the person
> hasn't just lost someone the night before, that they
> aren't suffering from a heart problem or a mental
> illness, and also that they understand what a psychic

reading is. We need to ensure that they know what's going to happen and that they aren't going to be traumatized by it.'

Natalie

'Doorstep divination is a real test for Derek – nothing's prepared, he's going in cold and yet he comes up with so much information, it's unbelievable.'

Angus

Now we have taken doorstep divination a step further and done it live! I was so excited to be part of it.

'The best thing is doing the doorstep divination live – we have no control over it at all. It's the most stomach-churning thing, because it's all on live TV and you just don't know who's going to answer the door.'

Natalie

Our first live show was in York in January 2006 – and we certainly weren't disappointed!

Where are we now?

> **'In less than eight months since the show has been
> commissioned, we've completed two series and two
> live shows, and the third series is about to start … It's
> an exciting journey we're all on and it's been an
> amazing adventure for all of us.'**
>
> Paul

At the time of writing, I have just completed the second live
show, which took place in Halifax. The second series is on
air and a third series is underway. The show is going from
strength to strength and I'm loving every moment of it!

Wherever we've been, we've had fun, had fascinating
experiences and, I hope, helped people to understand the
world of spirit. Our 'open-minded sceptic' has certainly had
a lot of food for thought.

> **'It's hard to be sceptical, because Derek can often prove
> you wrong. And in a way it's easy to dismiss things and
> it's often more difficult to believe, because then you
> have to work out *why* something's happening and
> what it means.'**
>
> Angus

But where next? My mediumship has already taken me to America, Canada and New Zealand, and I would love to take this show there too – and even further afield. It has already been sold to Canada, the United States and Iceland.

> **'*Ghost Towns* is a roller-coaster ride of a show and the fun's only just begun ... Our aim is to take Derek to the world – and beyond! – and to keep the Ghost Truck rolling.'**
>
> Paul

As for the future, we'll see. But now, let's go back to the very first series that went out on air…

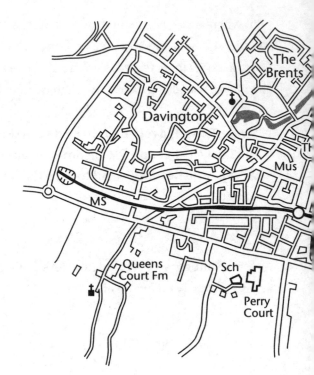

'I'd heard that Faversham had a lot of stories,
a lot of spiritual activity. I was expecting something.
I wasn't quite expecting this much.'

Angus

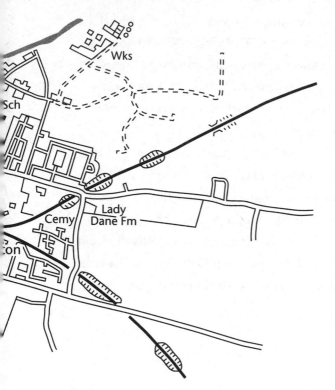

Chapter One

Faversham

As I arrived at Faversham, I wondered what spirits still haunted these old streets. The ancient Kentish town lies between the Downs and the sea. One of the famous Cinque Ports, it has a picturesque market square, a traditional brewery and many fine historic houses. But what else would we find there?

The Ghost Truck arrived at about nine in the morning and it wasn't long before it was packed with residents telling stories of strange phenomena and ghostly sightings. By midday we had hundreds of reports. There were many haunted places to choose from for our investigation, but when the Ghost Towns team heard the legend of a local pub, the Shipwright's Arms, they knew we had to start there.

The Shipwright's Arms

'I felt really privileged to be part of that, with that activity going on.'

Danniella

Neil Cole, who lives at the Shipwright's Arms, and Honda Rye and Trisha Philpot, who work there, told the Ghost Towns team that there had been many strange events in the old pub. A customer had disappeared right in front of the barmaid's eyes, a gas lamp had flown across the room, mysterious phone calls had been made from the pub when no one was there – it just went on and on. The level of activity had been constant over a long period of time and had been witnessed by many people.

Even as we were in the Ghost Car travelling to the pub I found I was picking up energy. It often happens that as I approach a property I am able to start sensing the energies present. If there is negative energy there, I feel a kind of anxiety or depression and know I have to prepare myself. In this case, I could feel a pull of psychic energy and I knew we were going to encounter spiritual activity.

Once we had arrived at the pub and been made welcome, we decided the easiest way to find out what was happening would be to hold a séance.

Séances

The word *séance* is French for a 'sitting'. A séance is when a group of people gather together to make contact with a spirit or spirits. It is not absolutely necessary for an experienced medium to be present, but I always consider it to be advisable. The people taking part in the séance arrange themselves in a circle, often around a table, place both feet on the floor and either hold hands or, if a table is being used, place their hands palms down upon it with the little finger of each hand touching the little finger of their neighbour on either side to form a chain of energy.

It is often a good idea to place a lighted candle in the centre of the table, as the flickering of the flame can indicate a spirit's movement through the atmosphere.

Everyone then closes their eyes and empties their mind of all thoughts, whilst the medium recites a prayer of invocation and protection for both themselves and the people taking part in the séance. Protection is highly important, as it is impossible to predict what sort of spirit or spirits will come to the group. Before I start any kind of psychic work I always perform an 'opening up' meditation to ask for protection from any negative energies. I call this my 'spiritual waterfall' and I visualize white light cascading down on me and protecting me from any negative energies.

During a séance, once contact with the spirit world has been made it is no longer absolutely necessary to maintain physical contact with the neighbouring person and people may rest their hands on their lap or on the tabletop if they wish, palms upwards to keep the energy field of the physical body open.

Although the medium leads the communication with the spirit or spirits, anyone can talk to them or ask questions of them. Participants are also encouraged to say how they are feeling at any time and to just go with the experience.

A séance should end with the medium 'closing the circle down' by thanking the spirits for their presence and offering a prayer of thanks and protection to help them to return to the spirit realms.

Séances can be a very useful way of getting in touch with the spirits who are present in a certain place and finding out more about them. At the Shipwright's Arms, this certainly proved to be the case.

The séance at the Shipwright's Arms

We sat around a table in the oldest part of the pub, lit a candle and all held hands. Once we had opened the circle, it wasn't long before I made contact with a spirit presence. I just wanted to scream out, 'Splice the main brace!' I took a deep breath and asked my spirit guide Sam to help him to step back. He was an angry spirit.

At that point I became aware of a strong smell of tobacco. 'He's got boxes and boxes and boxes of tobacco,' I said. 'He's piling it up. That's what he did.'

Who was he? I knew he was a strong man, but a weary man. He was a man of the sea. The reason he kept coming back to the pub was that he resented the way he'd lost his life. Sam told me that he'd barely made it this far. His ship had gone down, but he had not perished with it. He had got out of the water, but after that he had been walking blindly. He had had no idea where he was going.

The overpowering smell of tar...

The smell of tobacco was overwhelming. I had to ask Sam to back it off. I couldn't believe that no one else could smell it.

Then I caught a whiff of another smell.

'Ugh!' I wrinkled my nose.

'That's amazing,' said Angus, who was sitting on my right. 'That's horrible!'

'Can you smell it now?' I asked.

'I can smell it,' he said.

It was the smell of tar. It began wafting around the room and soon everyone started to smell it.

'When I first smelled the smells I just thought, "Oh, it's probably all in the mind," but it was really, really strong. I could really smell the tar. It was just like roads being laid.'

Trisha

'That happens all the time,' Neil said, 'and it's always around this area.'

Then I got a name: Frederick Symes. 'That's his name,' I stated.

'My favourite part of this investigation was actually putting a name to the sailor.'

Neil

Hardly had I said the words than Angus looked puzzled and asked, 'What's started swinging?'

Everyone looked up, startled. A lamp that was hanging above the bookshelf behind us was rocking back and forth. Its moving shadow was what had caught Angus's attention.

'That's got to be phenomena,' I explained. 'No one's touched it.' I felt really pleased that we were getting such a good response. 'Come on,' I said encouragingly, 'give it a really good swing!'

Suddenly Danniella exclaimed, 'That's moving, that one, that's moving as well!' She and Angus both pointed at once. A miner's lamp which was hanging near the other lamp was also swinging gently. The spirit man was responding to us.

'When we saw the lamps moving, we all stopped in our tracks.'

Angus

There was no window, no draught, no breeze, no physical reason why the lamps should be moving, and the wonderful thing about it was the way that the momentum kept up. There was no one near the lamps anyway, but if they had been physically pushed, sooner or later they would have slowed down and come to a stop, but the pace remained the same for six or seven minutes.

While we were still gazing at the swinging lamps, there

was a sudden thud near the bookcase. Angus jumped and turned towards the noise. 'Did you hear that?' he said. 'Like a thud on the floor.' Everyone had heard it.

Danniella was still looking at the miner's lamp, screwing her eyes up. 'That really is moving, isn't it? It's not just me, is it?'

We could all see the base of the miner's lamp moving slowly from side to side.

Then Trisha noticed something else. 'That book, that's just moved out as well.'

'It has!' I cried. 'It *has*! You are right!'

A book on the top shelf had moved forward, just as if a hand had pulled it towards the edge of the shelf.

'That was totally unexpected. You don't expect books to move out of line when they've all been in a perfect line... Yeah, that was strange, very strange.'

Trisha

'Thank you,' I said. 'Thank you for doing that.' The old sailor was really showing us that he was still around!

All this time the lamps were still moving. The first lamp was now moving randomly round and back again rather than swinging from side to side.

'I just had to smile. I knew that the old captain, as I call him, was going to show that he was still around.'

Honda

Danniella was curious. 'Neil, how does that make you feel? You live here.'

Neil wasn't bothered by it. 'It's fine,' he said. He smiled and shrugged. 'He's never done anything to me.'

I knew he never would.

Having succeeded in communicating with the spirit, we decided to finish the séance. I thanked everyone for their participation and closed the circle down.

When we looked up again, the lamps had stopped moving.

I was thrilled. In all my years I had never been in an investigation where I had got three responses like that in a matter of minutes. And, as Danniella said, the fact that the phenomena stopped once the séance was over was also interesting, as it showed that the energy had just backed right away.

Neil was amazed at what had happened in his pub. 'It was totally unexpected, because I've lived here for so long now and nothing's ever happened like that, ever, and it was amazing. I couldn't believe it.'

I found out afterwards that according to local legend, one Christmas Eve the captain of an old Dutch barge had been taken ill and had come banging on the door of the Shipwright's Arms. The bar manager at the time had thought it was a punter trying to get back into the pub and hadn't opened the door. When he did open it the following morning, he found the captain's body lying there. He had frozen to death during the night.

'We can tell them the real story now,' Trisha said, laughing.

The parapsychologist's view

Dr Simon Sherwood from the University of Northampton has been examining our results from a scientific perspective.

'There was no question that the lantern was definitely moving from side to side. One possible explanation is that the wooden beam that the lantern was suspended on was contracting due to the temperature cooling down and this may have caused it to move from side to side. So that's something that we would need to rule out. I actually measured the temperature along the beam that it was suspended on and found that there was indeed a temperature difference along it.'

'As for the book, I spoke to the landlord earlier and he said that very often when he goes to bed at night and locks the place up everything's in order and he comes down in the morning and finds that some of the books have been taken off the shelves and arranged in particular formations on the table. So it's interesting that that happened on the same shelf. I don't have a definite explanation.'

The local historian's *view*

'When we are doing our initial research into a town we will always come across the name of a noted local historian, and usually they are glad to help. We try to get the main local authority if we can, or if not, someone they have recommended. They come from a variety of backgrounds – they can be people who run museums, retired academics, and so on – but their local knowledge is always invaluable to us.'

Natalie

In the case of Faversham, the local historian was a gentleman called Dr Arthur Percival. He told us:

> 'The building was opened by a shipwright who had a yard there building sailing barges and, partly for his workforce and partly for people living in the area, he decided to open a beer house. Undoubtedly he did a very good trade with seafarers of various kinds and therefore it's possible that somebody, some seafarer, turned up and was turned away. You know, it's a feasible thing, certainly.'

The Crouch Family Home

'My name's Jo and I live in Faversham. And I believe our house is haunted.'

Jo Crouch

Mother and daughter Janet and Jo Crouch are part of a local Spiritualist circle, so are familiar with spirits – they even have several at home! They told us their house was haunted by a little girl and three boys. 'Tommy's a bit mischievous,' Janet explained, 'and he runs up and down stairs and shakes stepladders.'

'And their father's there as well,' Jo went on, 'and there's a lady in the bathroom. She's rather strict sometimes.' This definitely seemed a place worth investigating!

We met Janet and Jo in their dolls' house shop and as they led Danniella and me through to their home, I was hit by the atmosphere. A whole congregation of energies was coming in! We went up the stairs to the first floor and as we paused outside the bathroom I was aware that a lot of psychic activity had been going on there.

As the ladies themselves were so sensitive to spirit, Danniella suggested that we went straight into a circle to see what we could pick up. I thought that was an excellent idea.

There were so many spiritual energies there that someone was bound to communicate in one way or another.

Spirit communication

The spirit world is on a much faster vibration than ours – that's why most people can't pick spirits up. A medium has learned how to slow these vibrations down so that they can see and hear spirits more clearly. Spirits, too, have to learn how to slow down their vibrations in order to communicate. Those who have recently passed may not have learned how to do it yet and in these cases Sam passes their messages to me.

Spirits who are not able to communicate directly for one reason or another may be able to show their presence by a particular smell, perhaps a favourite perfume or the smell of something they were associated with – such as the tobacco and tar of Frederick Symes at the Shipwright's Arms – or by sending a 'psychic breeze' swirling past.

Some spirits can only pass on odd phrases. These can sound like snatches of conversation and you have to try to piece them together. Others can't express themselves in words at all, so they pass on emotions and sensations instead. Sometimes these can be highly unpleasant, especially if the spirit is showing how they died, but they all have a purpose, and that is to communicate with the living.

At the Crouchs' home, the first spirit that came through made himself known initially by a tight feeling across my chest. It was really painful. Then I saw him working with a hammer and metal. He was a proud and hardworking man, a strong man with thick-set arms.

> **'I had a strong vision of barrels, so we're pretty sure he must have worked in the brewery at some point.'**
>
> Janet

He had passed to spirit after a sudden heart attack at work. The pain I had felt was his way of showing me what had happened. I knew he was at the Crouchs' home regularly but he was a spirit in visitation, not a grounded spirit.

Spirits in visitation

Some spirits aren't in this world all the time but just pop in now and again for a visit. They often come to see loved ones or to visit places that were important to them in life.

Grounded spirits

Grounded or 'earthbound' spirits are those who stay on Earth after they have left their physical bodies rather than move on to the spirit realms.

There are many reasons why this can happen. Sometimes spirits don't realize they have passed. They may have died very suddenly, perhaps in an accident, and not understand what has happened to them. They may be very young and confused and so they don't go into the light. They remain here, often in a very bewildered state. They can't understand why people aren't taking any notice of them, so they make noises or move objects and try to draw attention to themselves.

Other spirits know they have passed over but are afraid to move on because they have performed wicked deeds and they know they will go to the lowest of the seven spirit realms. This isn't a nice place. It isn't the Christian idea of hell, with fire and brimstone, but it is a place where they will receive the justice they may have escaped on Earth. So they prefer to stay where they are.

Other spirits may have suffered some injustice in their lives and want to stay to see justice done. Sometimes justice *has* been done but they are not aware of it and they remain in a state of limbo.

Suicide is another reason why a spirit might not move on. Some people believe they will be punished if they take their own life, so again they are afraid to go into the light when they pass. In fact suicides are helped towards understanding and healing in the spirit realms – this may be a painful process, but it is not meant as a punishment.

Whatever reason has led to a spirit being grounded, if they
wish to move on, I can help them to do so. This is a very
important part of my work as a medium. During the *Ghost
Towns* investigations, if I find that a spirit is trapped I will
always help it to move on. The cameras may not always
show this, but it is always done.

'My name is Alice, my name is Alice.' It was a quiet spirit
voice in my ear.

'Who are you, Alice?' I asked.

'Oh, I feel so weird,' Janet said suddenly. 'Really sad.' She
was breathing heavily, almost breaking into sobs.

'Is it a lady?' Danniella asked.

'Yes, it's a lady.' After a while Janet gathered herself
together and went on, 'She can't leave. In her life she
couldn't leave. She was confined here. She's so sad…'

'What's the reason for her sadness?' Danniella was
concerned.

'They won't let her out.'

'Who?' we asked.

'It's her family.'

Then the spirit stepped back. That was all she could
communicate for now.

The next moment we all heard a knock. Spirit activity was
coming thick and fast now. Jo heard whispering in her ear
and was aware of spirit energies swirling around her. She

had talent as a medium and I encouraged her to develop this further in a safe and disciplined way. Janet assured me that that was what they had been doing.

We closed the circle, pleased with the results of our combined efforts. The effects of the energy were still being felt. Danniella felt as though she had a spider crawling down her neck, while Janet was really hot. She wiped her brow.

'Your hands are really hot,' Danniella told her.

She nodded. 'The amount of energy that's coming – it's just enormous.'

'The best part of the investigation for me was confirming things that we already felt and saw. Derek's just confirmed what we already felt, but his energy was so strong and he came through with much more detail than we picked up before. So that was good.'

Janet

'It was a great opportunity for three mediums, of different levels, to work together.'

Natalie

Doorstep Divination

'As soon as I opened the door, I thought it was a wind up.'

Barry Hunt

As we were on our way back from the Crouchs' home to the Ghost Truck, I felt a sudden pull towards a property. As we carried on down the road, the feeling lessened. 'Can we turn around?' I asked.

'You got a feeling, you gotta go with it!' said Danniella.

We got out and went up to the house. It was a former pub. This was our very first doorstep divination. Someone was about to get a big surprise!

'With the doorstep divination what amazes me is people's reactions. They have no idea we are coming and yet most of them are so calm – and they let us in. Why would you just let an unknown group of people into your house – with cameras?'

Natalie

A pleasant-looking middle-aged man opened the door. He was casually dressed and had probably been enjoying a quiet evening at home. Danniella quickly explained who we were and asked if I could do a reading. Looking rather shocked, the man said, 'Hang on a minute,' and motioned for us to stay on the doorstep while he stepped back into the house.

After a brief pause he returned with his wife, a slender brown-haired lady. She was polite but not too keen to get involved. 'Well, I'll stay out of it but you can do it,' she said to her husband. Rather cautiously, he agreed.

> **'To start with I was not too sure, because I'm extremely sceptical. But I thought, well, it wasn't going to hurt.'**
>
> Barry

Sitting on a sofa with Barry in the couple's elegant home, with Danniella looking on, I had the very strong impression that Barry was entering a phase of redirection – not spiritually, but in his day-to-day life. 'It could be in your business affairs,' I told him. 'I know it's been very tiring and it seems as though you can't find much time for relaxation.'

Barry blinked at me from behind his round glasses, looking rather bemused.

A man from the world of spirit was drawing close to us. Sam told me it was Barry's uncle. This gentleman had suffered problems with his heart. But did any of it mean anything to Barry?

'Alarmingly, quite a lot!' He was smiling, but was obviously quite surprised at what was taking place. He shook his head in amazement.

'He didn't know anything about me, didn't know what I do – and still doesn't – but there were certain things there that only somebody who knows me and knows what I do should know.'

Barry

'Who's Peter?' I continued. 'Not in spirit, I'm talking about business, people you know.'

Barry thought for a minute. 'There is a Peter I know,' he confirmed.

The spirits were telling me that Peter would have unbelievable news for Barry in the next couple of days. 'Watch for the telephone connection!' I told him. A little unsure, he smiled and nodded.

A woman in spirit was making herself known, someone who had suffered a great loss of body weight before her passing. 'There was somebody, yes,' Barry agreed.

This woman was pouring out feelings of affection and motherly love towards Barry. Along with the other souls gathered there, she had come because he had felt he had had the world on his shoulders and was battling on alone. Now I understood why I had been drawn to this house. I had to show Barry that there were people in the spirit world who were behind him, supporting him through this difficult time.

The spirit people had been listening in on conversations about having to rearrange a youngster's education. I had Barry's full attention now. His bright brown eyes rarely left my face. He smiled rather ruefully as he accepted what I was saying. 'Oh God!' He ran his fingers through his hair.

The spirit people were pleased with what he had done. 'You've done very well there,' I told him.

'I hope so!' he replied with a grin. Though he was smiling, I was aware that it had been a serious matter and of great concern to him.

'Mentioning education was a bit of a sore point. We're going through some interesting stages with my son and we've had some issues that we've had to deal with with his education – which are now dealt with. And that was the second lot of goosebumps, I think, because that was very recent.'

Barry

'Is there someone known to you called Susan?' I asked.

'Well, yes,' Barry replied. 'My wife's name is Susan.'

A lovely spirit lady had come to me, wanting to connect with Susan. She told me that she had been talking about getting involved in a course or some study linked with a course of some kind, but there had been hold-ups and she hadn't been able to move forward with her plans. I was pleased to be able to say that the obstacle would soon be removed.

Moving on to his home, the spirit people told me Barry had been having trouble with some pipework and had got quite frustrated with it – well, irate in fact!

He chuckled. 'There's something I can't find the source of,' he said quietly.

The spirits were telling me they could.

'Can they tell *me*, because I need to know!' Barry said, laughing.

Then I was shown a picture of the source. I explained to Barry where to look. I knew things were soon going to fall into place for him and that he had support from a lovely group of people in the spirit world.

'It's amazing,' he said as the reading came to an end. 'I mean, there's a lot there that I've been able to associate with. There was enough there to make the goosebumps rise!'

'Was there?' I was delighted that our first doorstep divination had been such a resounding success.

'I'm very pleased he came and did it. It's easy to say no to these things, but it was intriguing!'

Barry

Later I found out what happened next. Very soon after our visit Barry had gone on holiday to America for two weeks and when he returned, to his amazement, he had a water bill which ran into thousands of pounds. The pipework problem was proving no joke, but following the spirits' directions Barry soon found the source of the problem and it even turned out to be the fault of the water board.

'I'm even more pleased that Derek came now,' he said, 'because he's saved me so much money!'

Via Mystica Shop

'There's been a dark energy that's quite negative round there. We're sort of ... a bit frightened of it.'

Carol Rogers

Via Mystica is an alternative health shop that may once have been part of a medieval great hall. Mandy, Carol, Carol and Jean, a group of friendly mature women who all work there, told us about the Roman soldiers with no eyes who drifted through the wall, the shadowy figure that rushed by, the customers who had seen ghosts, the ley line that ran through the back of the shop to the toilet...

'The experiences that people had in the shop were all quite different. There were Roman soldiers, there was a lady in white, there were dark forces. And we thought, "Well, how can all these things be in this one shop?"'

Natalie

Angus and I went to investigate.

In the shop we were welcomed by the staff. Straightaway Sam told me to go to the back of the shop, where there was a portal, a vortex. This is a place where spirits enter and exit

this world. To us, it is a spot which can feel either hot or
cold.

We went out of the back of the shop and down a corridor
into a small room where stock and other items were stored
on shelves. 'This is it!' I said excitedly. 'This is the room
where energy is coming in and going out. The vortex is so,
so, so strong here.'

We were all standing packed together in the small room
and I was picking up information about a spirit man who
came in visitation. I explained that he would probably cause
the sensation of a person rushing past as he went in and out
of the portal. However, the stooped shadowy figure that
had often been seen in the area, rushing by at speed, was a
different spirit, one that went back to a different time frame.

'Was this ever part of an inn?' I asked. I was seeing wooden
tables and stools and smelling ale. It was the 1400s. This
was the period in which the shadowy figure had lived. She
was a lady whose life had been taken from her in the
cruellest way. I could see it all in front of me. I turned away
in horror. 'Take that picture, take it away from me!' I said to
Sam. I could see the woman being cut up, virtually
dismembered, during a ceremony, while a group of people
stood there chanting. I could also pick up on all her feelings
as this despicable act was being carried out. It was horrific. I
knew it had happened nearby and when her spirit had left
her body it had rushed back to the spot where the shop now

stood. Despite her traumatic death, the lady had moved on to the spiritual realms, but she still came back and relived her sadness, because she had never forgiven the perpetrators of that terrible deed and was still searching for them, seeking for justice.

'Sam,'I said,'try to explain to her that revenge is not the way! She's tormented!'

Angus told me then that four witches had been killed publicly in Faversham in some kind of horrid ceremony.

I knew just how awful it had been.'They bled her,'I explained'they slit her and bled her to death and then did despicable things afterwards to her physical body and she's coming through wanting justice.'

I knew that by now the evil souls involved would have received their just reward, but their victim wouldn't have been aware of this and wouldn't have been able to find them in the spirit world because they wouldn't be in the same realm. Such evil people would have gone straight to the lowest spirit realm and might still be there, because until they repented of their deeds they wouldn't be able to progress. I asked that they would one day see the error of their ways and that this poor soul would be helped to let go of the past and find peace.

> **'I was being prodded in the back all the time this was
> going on and I didn't like to say anything, as I didn't
> want to disturb Derek ... I thought it was the
> cameraman, to tell me to move, then I realized that
> he was standing on the wrong side of me, so it
> couldn't possibly have been him.'**
>
> Carol Rogers

This experience had been harrowing to me as a medium,
but I left Via Mystica knowing that although terrible things
had happened nearby in the past, the shop itself was a
peaceful place. It will always have spirits there, moving in
and out of the vortex, but most of them will be lovely souls
just passing through.

> **'When Derek came to the shop it was a wonderful
> experience ... We were very, very impressed by what
> he found for us.'**
>
> Jean Webb

Faversham **Brewery**

> '**The brewery is definitely haunted and from the stories I've been told and the feelings I get I think the ghosts are definitely malevolent. I think they're quite nasty.**'

Mark Stiff

Faversham Brewery is a important part of the town. Built on the site of a former monastery, over the years it has been a major employer, but many people came to the Ghost Truck to tell us that they would not set foot in it because of the dark spirits said to lurk there.

One current employee, Mark, a down-to-earth man with flowing locks, offered to show us around. Danniella, Angus and I couldn't wait.

> '**Faversham's famous for its brewery and loads of people coming to the truck were telling us about the experiences that they had had there, but they were too scared to go back and investigate, so we were thrilled when Mark said that he would.**'

Natalie

As we were in the Ghost Car travelling towards the brewery, I started to get a feeling of apprehension. By the time we arrived, it had turned to dread.

At the brewery we met up with Mark and as we made our way through the twisting brick corridors to the malt kiln, I was immediately aware of a group of monks walking four or five deep. Sam told me that they were Benedictines. These spirits were roaming all over the brewery, concerned about a lost soul.

The local historian's *view*

'There was a Faversham Abbey, of course, which was a Benedictine abbey. He was spot on there.'

Dr Arthur Percival

The malt kiln was dark and creepy…

At that point Danniella decided that as the brewery was so large it might be a good idea to leave Angus in the malt kiln and take me to a different part of the brewery to see if I could pick up the story better elsewhere.

'Am I on my own here?' asked Angus nervously. 'Just don't close the door then!'

We told him all he had to do was holler and we would come back to him. Danniella left him with a camera and we walked off.

'I'm not very keen on being in the dark – which is something I wasn't really that aware of until I started working with Derek. But in the dark I just lose my co-ordination. I suffer from claustrophobia too. And though the night-vision cameras show quite clearly what's happening, we really can't see at all.'

Angus

'The malt kiln room, the room we left Angus in, was horrible. It was dark, it was dense, it was wet, it was horrible – just a horrible room! Very, very dark – you couldn't see a thing in front of you. It didn't have a good feeling to it at all.'

Danniella

But it wasn't long before Danniella was having her own problems. As we followed Mark through the brewery and across an area where bags of grain were piled up, she asked worriedly, 'This isn't the place with the rats, is it?'

'No,' he reassured her, 'it's just the place with the mice.'

'Oh no, don't say that!'

As we carried on walking, I saw something. 'Oh yes, there are a few of them here, a couple just ran across there, look!'

'Shut *up*!' Danniella wailed. She stood stock still.

'Look, there were only a couple of them, Danniella, a couple of them just ran across.'

'No! I'm goin'! I'm out of here!'

'They were just running, they weren't *jumping*.'

'No, I'm out of here! Honestly! I don't do mice! Or rats!' She turned away and wouldn't go on.

'Derek, please, you go.'

'Look, you just hold my hand…'

'No, you go, just go.' She stood still and wouldn't move. 'I don't do mice!' she repeated. She put her hands up to her face. 'I can't, I can't do it.'

It took quite a lot of persuading before she finally allowed me to take her hand and lead her forward. Huddling in her coat, with her eyes firmly shut, her head down and her other hand over her eyes, she followed me through the area with the grain and into the malt silos, where we were safe from mice. I did feel sorry for her, but I couldn't help but feel just a tiny bit amused that in a brewery full of spirits, what bothered Danniella was a couple of small furry animals!

In the malt silo I was soon picking up the energies of a spirit man. I could feel that he was being engulfed by something and was having problems with his breathing, but I didn't know what was around him at first – it wasn't water, but what was it? Something was raining down on him from above, suffocating him. I tried to understand what was happening to this man. One thing I knew for sure was that he wasn't in visitation: he was trapped.

I asked him to come forward and tell us who he was.

Almost straightaway Sam gave me his name: Edward Stimpson.

Then we asked his age. Sam told me that he was 26 years old. Then I knew what had happened! He had been testing the grain when he had slipped, overbalanced and fallen in.

As I related this to Mark and Danniella, we heard a plopping sound in an area behind us. I asked whether it could be some kind of machinery, but Mark said no, there was nothing there. Was it Edward Stimpson communicating with us? We decided to move towards the area where we'd heard the noise.

I reminded the spirit that we were his friends and respected him. Then I suggested he make a noise above us.

'There you go!' said Danniella at once. She had heard a noise at the end of the hall.

She asked Mark to talk to the spirit. He too asked Edward to make a noise.

We all waited in anticipation. Then there came a distinct couple of raps, much louder than before.

'Hear that bang?' I said to Mark. 'That was heavy. Ask him again.'

At that moment, unbeknown to us, in the dark back in the malt kiln Angus heard a scraping sound.

'What the hell was that?' Startled, he looked down to his left.

It came again and then seemed to come from the other side of him. Angus looked round in alarm. 'What the hell was that noise?' he whispered.

We were also hearing noises – bangs and thumps and what sounded like a creaking door that suddenly slammed. Each sound was getting closer to us. It seemed that the spirit trapped in the brewery was responding to Mark's requests.

'Tell him to come closer,' I said.

Mark did so and once more we waited with baited breath.

Then there was a tap.

The spirit was continuing to respond.

'Come closer, come closer to Derek. Keep making the noise,' said Mark.

The parapsychologist's *view*

'Yes, there were noises. I don't think there was any evidence there to suggest that they were paranormal.'

Dr Simon Sherwood

Then I felt the energy swirling around me. I swayed and closed my eyes. Once more I asked the spirit to come closer. I had a feeling at the back of my shoulders. Then with a shiver I was channelling the man who had died in the grain silo.

Channelling

Channelling is a way of allowing a spirit to communicate by entering the auric field of a medium. Our auric field surrounds our physical body, protecting us. A spirit person cannot penetrate it unless we give them permission. In Faversham Brewery I had repeatedly asked the spirit to come close to me, but if I had said no, he couldn't have jumped in. I make my own decisions on when to channel a spirit and follow Sam's advice about whether a spirit is trustworthy or not. Having said this, once or twice I've misjudged the situation and a cunning spirit has leapt in and taken advantage of the opportunity. Fortunately, this doesn't happen often.

When I let a spirit enter my body, it is as if I step to one side. I know words are being spoken through my physical body, but I can't hear them clearly. Sometimes I am completely unaware of what is happening to my physical body. I feel cold, because my spirit is out of its housing, and dislocated. It doesn't feel right.

Mediums can't be possessed, as we have the spiritual resources to come back into our own bodies, but if ever the people around me when I am channelling are disturbed by what is happening and feel that things have gone too far, my tour manager Ray will come and say, 'Derek, come forward.' That will always bring me back. On *Ghost Towns*, I am only allowed to channel for four minutes for safety reasons.

Sometimes it takes a while to recover from the experience. If the spirit's energy has been negative, I can feel tired for several days afterwards and even lose my appetite and have problems sleeping.

As I was channelling, I wasn't aware of what was happening to my body. It was a blank to me, but Danniella and Mark were amazed to see me shuffle towards the wall, with an odd gait totally unlike my own, and stand there with my head down. At first I seemed to be groaning and no one could make out what I was saying, but then it became clearer: 'Eleanor, Eleanor!'

Slowly I raised my arms above my head and threw my head back, crying out the name over and over, but still groaning and gasping as though I was being suffocated.

Danniella rushed across to me. As I fell backwards, my arms still in the air as if to protect my face, she caught me and then Ray ran over to me and helped her to lie me flat on the floor. I was gasping and choking and making ugly gurgling noises. Mark looked on in horror.

'I was so shocked. I should have helped the man really, but I was just so shocked to see him collapse and luckily Danniella was there to pick him up before he hit the floor.'

Mark

'It was fantastic to see – very sad, but fantastic – and when he collapsed back on to me, before Ray stepped in, it didn't worry me, it didn't bother me in the slightest, because I knew it wasn't a bad spirit, it wasn't anything horrible. This man was just trying to show what had happened to him.'

Danniella

'Come forward, come forward,'Ray called.

At that I came back into my body, still coughing and choking, and Ray pulled me up into a sitting position. Everyone looked shocked and concerned, but I knew I was alright. Breathing heavily, I rested for a few moments.

'Ray's very much part of the team. He's always in the room and is the first port of call when Derek's channelling. He helps out the production team in many ways and is a great person to have around – he's a very safe pair of hands.'

Natalie

Ray helped me to my feet and we moved away from the area where the poor young man had lost his life so tragically.

'Oh my God, bless him,'I said.'Oh my, the poor soul.'I felt such sympathy for the man who had died in such a horrible manner.

'Shall we leave here?'Danniella asked. Mark nodded.

'It was unbelievable. To witness something like that was amazing, it really was.'

Mark

The parapsychologist's *view*

> '**Derek was apparently re-enacting the last moments of the man who suffocated in the silo. It's possible that he became quite absorbed in the idea that the person had suffocated and his brain came up with this other character, or that this was another aspect of Derek's personality that came through.**'

Dr Simon Sherwood

'Hello, darlin'!' Danniella greeted Angus with a smile. 'You look like you've been in the Blitz!'

Angus wasn't quite where we'd left him.

'I had to come out,' he explained. 'I was scared. I heard a noise and I felt as if I was trapped in a dungeon.'

> '**I stayed in there for as long as I could, but after a while I just thought, "I can't take this any more," and I heard a noise. I just don't know if I had tripped on something or if it was something else. I hope there was nothing else in there with me.**'

Angus

The investigation at Faversham Brewery had shaken us all. But we weren't going to let it put us off. It was time to pack up and set off down the road to the next ghost town.

'Everything I expected to happen did, and it was just better than I expected.'

Danniella

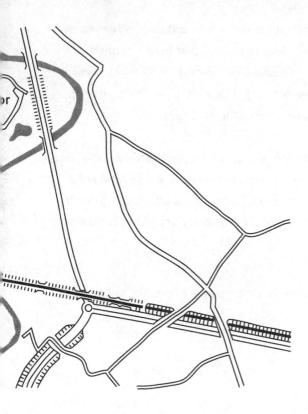

Chapter Two

Shrewsbury

Shrewsbury, the county town of Shropshire, is known as England's finest Tudor town. It is famous for being the former home of Charles Darwin and for its annual flower show. There also seemed to be a lot of psychic activity there. Was it about to be famous for its ghosts?

'Driving into Shrewsbury my expectations were high. Straightaway you notice there are so, so many old buildings, dark corners and dark alleyways. I don't think the people of Shrewsbury are living here alone.'

Angus

I was delighted to see that a crowd of people had turned out to welcome us.

'In Shrewsbury we actually had the town crier – the tallest town crier in the world, who is 7 ft 2 inches tall – out there with his bell crying, "Oh yea, oh yea, Shrewsbury welcomes you, *Derek Acorah's Ghost Towns*!" He was really bringing the people in!'

Natalie

It wasn't long before they were piling into the Ghost Truck to tell us their stories.

'As soon as you arrive, you realize what a historical place it is. But when people came to the Ghost Truck and started telling us their stories, we realized it was a spooky place as well.'

Natalie

The Parade Shopping Centre

> 'The shopping centre is one of the scariest places I personally have ever been in. I certainly wouldn't be left there on my own.'

Natalie

The Parade Shopping Centre is in one of the oldest parts of the town, at the top of Pride Hill. It is housed in a beautiful early nineteenth-century building. Sara and Melanie, two young women who worked there, came to the Ghost Truck to tell the team of the ghosts that still haunted its corridors.

Melanie mentioned a cold spot in her shop. These spots can indicate the vortices where spirits enter and exit our world. Strange noises had also been heard, including footsteps. Sara said that when she was coming out of a small washroom she had seen a shadowy figure that she thought was a woman. Angus and I set off to investigate.

> 'I was petrified in the Parade Shopping Centre. Downstairs was very creepy.'

Angus

On arriving at the shopping centre, I felt a sense of anticipation. The atmosphere was permeated with energies and almost at once I had a spirit lady shouting at me! I had to put my hands over my ears.'Stop it!'I told her.'Stop that!'

As Melanie and Sara looked on, I turned to Angus. There was another spirit lady there, asking me to put my hands on his shoulders, then to pass them across his chest. Angus looked a bit baffled at first and I felt the same.'What's she doing that for, Sam?'I asked. I knew she had a good intent, but I didn't know what it was. Sam told me she was just checking Angus out to make sure he was healthy.

Sara and Melanie started smiling when they heard that.

'Is she a nurse?'Angus asked me. I wasn't sure, but I knew she was concerned about people, wanted to look after them and was always on the go, up and down a certain corridor.

Angus turned to Sara and Melanie,'Because this used to be a hospital, didn't it?'

They nodded.

'There is a ghost that we all know about who is a matron.'

Sara Heller

It seemed that this was the spirit who was making herself known to us. She was just visiting, not a grounded spirit, but she was a very regular visitor.

'Why is she coming back, Derek?' Angus asked.

'She's coming back because she's…' I started.

'Checking on the patients,' Sara finished for me .

Yes, that was what she was doing!

She was talking to me but her voice was faint. 'Come on,' I said to her, 'say it again. I can't hear you.'

I listened carefully. 'It's either Molly or Polly,' I said. 'What is it, Sam? She's not getting through to me clearly.'

Then Sam gave me the name: Molly Evans.

It seemed that Molly was fine – she just popped back on a regular basis to check up on the former hospital. But who had been the first spirit, the one who had been screeching in my ear?

'I've heard other people who've got shops in here say that they've actually heard screaming at times,' said Melanie.

We decided to walk around the shopping centre to see if we could make contact with the distressed spirit.

Then I felt a psychic pull. I was being drawn to the women's toilet!

Melanie, Sara, Angus and I all crammed into the small space. Luckily the shopping centre was closed, so no one else would need to come in!

This was where the vortex was. I explained to Sara and Melanie that it was where the spirits were entering and exiting. As I was doing so, I noticed that Angus was looking round him rather uneasily.

'Is there anybody here, because I'm feeling a lot of cold on my hands,' he said.

The others agreed. 'Right behind me, it's ice cold,' said Melanie.

Angus walked behind her to check. 'That's cold, yeah,' he confirmed.

Spirits were present. I asked whether any of them would like to draw close to the ladies.

Melanie seemed to be affected straightaway. She started swaying. 'I feel as if someone's actually pushing me!' she said, wide eyed. 'As if they're pushing me against the wall!'

'When I was in the toilet I felt dizzy, light-headed, and then I felt this really strong pressure, as if somebody was pushing me very hard, and I kept falling against the wall. It was really strong pressure. I had really bad backache and I think that was because I was trying so hard to stand upright.'

Melanie Molineux

I went behind Melanie to feel the energy. It was phenomenal – not cold energy, but heat all around her shoulders. She was laughing with amazement and I knew she had the psychic strength to withstand the experience. She wasn't distressed but exhilarated by it.

As we were talking about the remarkable energy, Angus

suddenly said, 'What was that?' He pointed towards the ceiling. 'What was that scream?'

Everyone looked round. I had heard it too. It had sounded like a woman or a young person. We left the vortex and moved towards the area where the noise had come from.

As we were walking back down the corridor I felt some troubled energies. A young spirit lady was there, but she was holding back.

'Whenever I've been in here on my own at night it's always been that area that we were in that has felt cold and just wrong.'

Sara

'Come close, come close,' I said to the spirit lady. 'Encourage her, Sam.' Sam will always help with spirits who are a little shy or who don't find it easy to communicate. His help is invaluable to me.

I was trying to get what we call an 'audible reaction' from the spirit – and we certainly did get one! Hardly had I started talking to her than Melanie jumped and cried out and Angus shouted wildly, 'The mirror just moved, the mirror just moved!'

The mirror in question was in a wide frame and was standing on a small glass-topped table. Melanie had been standing to the left of it and I had been to the right. I had actually felt the movement of air myself, but had not seen what had caused it. Angus had been opposite it, which is why he had seen it happen.

'When that mirror moved in the shopping centre, I was just stunned. I was petrified. I just about shot out the door.'

Angus

'I felt something hit my hand or touch my hand. It was on my right-hand side, but it was either somebody tapping me – well, that's what it felt like – or it was the mirror moving, but it was a definite feeling on my hand, enough to make me jump and shout.'

Melanie

The parapsychologist's *view*

'I examined the mirror afterwards and the table on which it was placed. It was a free-standing mirror on a glass surface and the table wasn't particularly sturdy. Perhaps the mirror just slipped or somebody knocked the table or vibrations throughout the floor, through people moving around, caused the mirror to slip.'

Dr Simon Sherwood

Everyone stared at the mirror and started talking at once. I tried to restore calm. I thanked the spirit and asked her to do something again.

'Come and talk to us,' said Sara, gently. 'Let Derek know your name. How do you want us to help you?'

There was a moment's silence. Everyone waited anxiously for the spirit to make contact. Then I felt the energy coming around my shoulders and I bent my head. The spirit came close to me, into my auric field. I slumped to my knees, as if in prayer, and started channelling her.

> **'The highlight for me was watching Derek channelling Moira.'**
>
> Angus

The parapsychologist's *view*

> **'Channelling is where it is claimed that the spirit of a person is communicating directly through the medium. In terms of possible explanations for that, a truly sceptical person would say that the medium's just acting or making it up. Derek's explanation would be that he is channelling the spirit of a deceased person.'**
>
> Dr Simon Sherwood

I don't have any recollection of what happened next, but later Angus told me about it. He had knelt down beside me and been able to pick up a whispered name: 'Moira.'

'Is your name Moira?' asked Sara. 'What happened to you, Moira?'

'The cancer.'

'You've got cancer?' Angus asked. He and Sara looked at each other and then back towards me, concerned, as Moira gave a loud piercing wail.

'Moira, are you a patient here?' Angus asked. 'Are you here to recover?'

'They told me lies.'

'They told you lies? Who told you lies?' asked Angus.

'They said that you were going to be alright but you're not.' Sara had figured it out.

'Yes…'

Sara and Angus carried on asking questions.

'Are you still in pain, Moira?'

She was beating her chest frantically.

'Is there anything we can do to help you?'

'*Take it away*.'

'When Derek was channelling I was just worried for the girl that he was trying to move on. She obviously was in a lot of pain and very distressed.'

Sara

'Who lied to you in hospital?' Angus persisted.

'Was it the nurses?' Sara asked.

'Molly.'

'Molly?' Angus said. 'She told you you were going to be OK?'

'Yes, yes, yes … I can't move.'

'You can't move?'

'Help me, please!'

Moira was so upset that Ray intervened and brought me back. 'What did she say?' I asked.

Though it was not shown on camera, we then joined forces to help Moira on her way to her spiritual home at last.

> **'Now it feels a lot clearer and easier in that area. It doesn't feel as tight or cold.'**
>
> Sara

> **'It feels quite happy now – a comfortable feeling, you know. I don't feel worried about being in here any more.'**
>
> Melanie

Pengwerne Books

'When we went into the bookshop I was really surprised that Derek just changed and he said that it was a really evil spirit, a bad spirit.'

Danniella

The bookshop on the corner of Prince's Street had apparently been the scene of paranormal activity for some time. Books would fall off the shelves for no apparent reason and the staff had once watched astounded as a box shot across the floor by itself.

'Very often you would feel one side of your body go very cold,' June Watts, the former proprietor, recalled, 'almost ice cold.' She was convinced the shop had several spirits, including a number of children who had died in a fire, a servant who had hanged themself in the attic and a dark force that prowled the premises.

As Danniella and I entered the bookshop June herself greeted us. She was a quiet and pleasant middle-aged blonde lady. The atmosphere of the shop, however, was far from pleasant. In fact it was horrible. I began to feel apprehensive.

As we went up the stairs, the energy hit me. 'Wow!' It was a spirit man, pressing down on my shoulders.

> '**As we went up the steps he seemed to get the feeling of a man, a quite strong and angry man. It was quite spooky in a way because we hadn't talked about the man that was meant to be on the stairs or around that area. We had been told he was quite a nasty man, but as Derek said he wasn't nasty, he was just angry.**'
>
> June

The man wanted to push me away. He seemed to be very intolerant. I could hear him shouting at a group of children. They were spirit children and were scared of him. A single bell was chiming continually. I didn't know what it meant, but June explained that there used to be a church nearby.

The local historian's *view*

> '**The bookshop used to be the house of the sexton of old St Chad's church, across the road, and the church collapsed in spectacular fashion when the bells chimed at four o'clock in the morning on 9 July 1788, and it was the chiming of the bells that brought down the bell tower.**'
>
> Pam Roberts-Powis

While there was a lot of spirit movement at times on the landing, what we really needed was to get a conscious link with the man. We moved into June's former office, now an almost empty storeroom. She had experienced a lot of activity there and it wasn't long before I picked up on two spirit boys. There was also a little girl, who had died of a fever, perhaps consumption. These children had no family link to the intolerant man. I felt he had passed due to some kind of accident, perhaps before this building had been here.

'There was an accident,' June confirmed, 'a big fire.'

Could this account for all the activity that had been experienced in the bookshop or was there something else? Earlier on I had been drawn to a certain corner of the building and had wanted to go down. June explained that the building did have a cellar. We all went down to it.

'We call this "the well",' June said, leading the way into a small room with painted brick walls. 'We used to store stuff in it.'

The area was clean and neat, but the energy – it was horrible.

'When you first go in it seems very, very normal, but when you go through to the back, the atmosphere completely changes.'

Natalie

'I always avoided the well because I just didn't like going out there. It felt too creepy to me. Maybe it was because of the spirits.'

June

I put my hand to my head. 'Whoah!' It was a woman of evil intent – a witch who had practised the dark arts.

'Wow, where's that coming from, that freezing cold air?' Danniella was looking around, wondering why she felt a sudden chill.

'That's because we're talking about her.'

We all put our hands out and felt the cold air swirling around. I could also pick up the 'psychic smell' down there – it was absolutely putrid. The residual energy held the memory of the witch's passing – she had ended up in flames.

We could all feel the cold air

Residual energy

Intense emotional situations have a very strong energy which can be absorbed by the fabric of a building or a particular place and detected by a physically sensitive person. Scenes can be replayed, much like a videotape, under the right conditions.

I could see that this witch had been burnt and had suffered great agony, yet such was her evil that as she was dying she had not cried out for mercy, but had screamed curses instead, swearing vengeance on the people who had brought her to justice and all their family line. She had been a truly evil person – I felt sure she had been responsible for taking lives herself, particularly young lives.

Then I realized she hadn't worked alone – she had been the head of a group. Quickly I counted – there had been four, possibly five of them! I could see the sort of things they had got up to, and it was horrible. Dissection wasn't the worst of it.

'I've never experienced anything to do with witchcraft at all. That was my first ever experience and hopefully it'll be my last. I didn't like it.'

Danniella

The local historian's *view*

'After the collapse of the church there was a record that the font had to be secured against the activity of witches.'

Pam Roberts-Powis

I wasn't willing to make closer contact with this evil spirit, but we couldn't leave things as they were.

'Can we cleanse this space we're in?' asked Danniella.

June, Danniella and I all joined our energies by holding hands and I asked for the stench of darkness and evil to be lifted from that place. With the help of the spirit world, the atmosphere lifted and light came in. There wouldn't be any more trouble here now.

The Old Post Office Hotel

'You never really feel quite alone in there.'

Brendan Green

The staff at the Old Post Office Hotel were convinced that the beautiful Tudor building was haunted. Guinevere, Amy and Brendan came to the Ghost Truck to tell us about a variety of phenomena, including electrical equipment turning itself on and off and a mysterious ball of light moving around. Guinevere had once seen a shadowy figure behind her when she was in the bar, a chambermaid had been making the beds when an unseen person started tugging at the bedclothes, and Amy had been followed up the stairs by the smell of lavender.

  Angus and I set off to investigate.

  'The Old Post Office Hotel was a very big building and from the stories it seemed to be absolutely riddled with ghosts, so it was difficult to choose where to go. We let Derek take the lead and he took us up to a bedroom where he linked with a spirit.'

  Natalie

As soon as I opened the hotel door I became aware of energies, sad energies. First of all I led the way into a room where there was a definite spirit presence watching and listening to us. I could see clairvoyantly a man lifting the back leg of a horse and tending to it. I realized he had been a farrier and was re-enacting what he used to do.

The local historian's *view*

> **'The Old Post Office was a coaching inn, so yes, a farrier to shoe horses would have been an important role.'**
>
> Pam Roberts-Powis

Brendan told me he had heard a noise in the cellar which sounded as if it was a cart being pulled along and had assumed it was traffic. So it was – but traffic of long ago.

'Oh God, no!' I put my hands up to my neck and turned away. Something had been placed around my throat and was tightening and tightening.

A spirit lady was showing me what had happened to her – she had been strangled. I felt as if she had been raped first and then her attacker had decided to silence her to prevent his crime from coming to light.

'When Derek was mentioning the strangulation of the lady, that kind of scared me. I nearly pulled Brendan's trousers down at one point, to be perfectly honest. I had to hold his trouser leg at the back.'

Guinevere Wood

'I felt as if I had this heaviness about my legs. And I actually just felt drunk, kind of drunk and sick, and that's why I went over to sit on the bed. That was not an enjoyable experience.'

Angus

I wasn't really aware of the hotel staff clinging on to one another and Angus moving to the bed because I was concentrating on what had happened to the woman. Her body had been dragged across the cobbles and hidden in a small room. I knew we had to go out there.

Outside in the courtyard it was dark and there were several doors leading off to different parts of the building, but Sam led me to one particular door. I placed both hands on it.

'Please open this, will you? This is it.'

Amy and Guinevere looked on as Brendan opened the door for me.

We all entered a small room. This was where the poor woman's body had been kept.

'It was very dark and musty and not very pleasant at all. It was just a very small enclosed space.'

Danniella

'The most interesting part was when Derek took us out to our storeroom and told us about the lady being dragged across the cobbles. It was very strange. We'd never heard anything about that before.'

Amy Pugh

How close were we to running water?

'There's a river just at the bottom of the hill,'Brendan told me.

That was where the rapist had taken his victim's body. I felt certain he had covered it up and taken it away at night, in a cart, which was why cart noises were being heard to this day.

We decided to conduct a séance to see whether we could make contact with any of the spirits who were there. As we stood in a circle with our hands joined, I asked whether any spirits wished to draw near and touch one of us.

'My neck's really, really burning,'Brendan said straightaway.

A spirit was doing as we had asked – and by touching Brendan's neck she could be showing us that she was the woman who had lost her life when she had been strangled.

**'I had this burning sensation down my neck. It felt
as though a hot wire or something was being pulled
around the back of my neck. It was quite
uncomfortable. I've never experienced anything like
that before.'**

Brendan

'It's happening to my forehead,' said Amy. 'It's like a burning
on my forehead, a stabbing sort of pain.'

We stood still for a moment and then there came a sliding
sort of sound, rather indistinct, as if from a distance.

'Can you hear that?' said Angus nervously.

Danniella and I looked at each other.

'Does that sound like someone walking over the cobbles?'
I asked her. 'Or something being dragged?'

'Sounds like footsteps to me,' said Danniella.

I thought it was more of a constant sound. We held our
breath and concentrated, trying to work out what it was.

'Oh, can you hear that?' asked Angus again.

'It's really eerie!' exclaimed Danniella.

'It's like a knocking, isn't it?' I said.

'Girls, can you hear it?' Danniella asked. Amy and
Guinevere nodded.

'It's like footsteps across cobbles,' said Angus.

Brendan told us that this was the sound he had heard
before, when he was in the cellar.

Angus decided to try a new tack. 'Run your hands through Brendan's hair,' he said to the spirit.

'It feels as though somebody's got their hands on the back of my neck,' Brendan said.

I placed a hand around the back of his neck and could feel the energy.

'It's burning,' Brendan continued. 'It feels as though somebody's hand is rubbing it.'

The parapsychologist's *view*

'Often the role of the medium is almost like a hypnotic situation where the medium's making suggestions about what might happen, and people might respond to that suggestion, particularly if they really believe things are going to happen or if they believe the place is haunted.'

Dr Simon Sherwood

Then Danniella spoke to the spirit. 'Can you touch Brendan's face?' she asked. 'Can you stroke his face or his hand? Or maybe Amy? Can you do it to Amy?'

'It feels as if someone's stroking my face now,' said Amy at once.

**'I was touched on the face. It was very strange. I was
not expecting that at all.'**

Amy

'I can feel something blowing on the back of my neck,' said
Guinevere. She was standing next to Amy. It seemed that
the spirit lady was going round the circle, just making
herself known to us.

Guinevere turned her head and smiled.

'What can you feel?' asked Danniella.

'It's just tickling.'

Then Danniella herself started to feel it. 'It's like a spider
on me,' she said with an amused smile. 'On my crown. I
want to scratch it.'

**'As the spirit moved round the room and touched
people individually, just before it was my turn – and
I'm so glad nothing happened – I just about bolted.
That was really, really frightening.'**

Angus

Brendan could hear the knocking sound again. It seemed
as if it was coming from behind Danniella. Danniella,
Angus and I all felt that the spirit was responding well to
Brendan. 'Keep speaking, because she really likes you,'
said Angus.

Brendan asked the spirit whether she could make some noises on the cabinets in the room.

'Oh!' cried Angus. He stared at me, wide eyed. 'What the hell was that noise?'

It had been a thud somewhere behind us. We all looked round.

'Did you all hear that?' said Angus. 'Too much!'

The spirit was responding to us, but the energy was intense.

'I'm so dizzy,' complained Danniella.

I was starting to feel a little dizzy too, which was unusual for me.

Then Danniella started swaying. 'I don't feel very well,' she said. 'I'm not sure how much longer I can stay in here.'

'Maybe we should leave this atmosphere,' I suggested.

'It was quite eerie in that room because it was so cold, and I didn't like it – I'll be honest. I couldn't wait to leave.'

Guinevere

Brendan said his neck was still burning. 'It's really uncomfortable now.'

I explained that it would soon go, but in fact it didn't – instead the energy built up. I had to put my hands on the back of Brendan's neck and ask Sam to take the feeling away.

In spite of the intense energy, I knew the spirit didn't mean any harm. She had just returned to the scene of her horrible demise to make us aware of her sad story.

'I'm glad that Derek's been because he said that, you know, the spirit just comes in visitation and she doesn't mean any harm when she comes, and that's good to know. It puts your mind at rest a bit.'

Brendan

The Haunted Flat

> '**I just thought we were going to go in and find out what had gone on there and I didn't realize just how intense it was going to become.**'

Danniella

While the team had been checking out the Old Post Office Hotel they had heard about another haunted property.

> '**Dane was one of the bar staff at the Old Post Office and when he was working his girlfriend Melissa used to go and sit at the end of the bar because she was too scared to stay in their flat by herself. That convinced us to investigate!**'

Natalie

The next day Dane Wyton and Melissa Page came to the Ghost Truck to tell them more about it. They certainly had problems in their flat. Herb jars moved around. Glasses moved. Electrical appliances turned themselves on and off. A toast rack and ashtray had flown across the room towards Melissa. One night Dane's guitar had strummed itself. A radio in the kitchen had turned itself on. When asked to turn itself up, it had done so. When asked to turn itself down, it had switched itself off completely. There was such a horrible feeling in the bathroom that no one wanted to stay in there for long. In the bath one day Melissa had heard a tap on the window, but she knew there was no way anyone could reach the window ledge from outside. By now she was so scared she was thinking of moving out.

Even before we arrived at the flat, both Danniella and I felt the negative energy emanating from it. I was also picking up on the spirit of a man and I could feel my left eye being affected. As we stood outside the front door, I put my hand up to it. 'I don't feel good about this,' I said.

In the flat we were met by Dane and Melissa. This lovely young couple were obviously concerned about what was happening to them. I was determined to help them in any way I could.

Standing in the kitchen, I was aware of a spirit lady. She was taking me into an area where there was a lot of milk – it seemed to be a dairy of some sort. She was the wife of the man I had picked up earlier. She had been a hardworking woman who had helped her husband. They had worked as a team. But what was coming from her energies was nothing short of evil.

The local historian's *view*

'The property is in Milk Street and that's where the dairying activities of the town would have been concentrated.'

Pam Roberts-Powis

'I'm getting "J"…' I spelled the letters out in the air.
'DAVIES.'

'Is that the male or the female?' Danniella asked.

I didn't know yet, but I knew the woman wasn't happy. 'And he was a bit of a stubborn character as well,' I told Dane and Melissa. This was putting it mildly, to be honest, because I sensed that these were quite dark spirits.

The woman would have targeted Melissa. Had she ever noticed an unseen presence brushing past her or suddenly turned cold or felt an unexplained breeze? Melissa nodded.

The man, meantime, had made it his business to torment Dane. He would walk towards him and try to literally press him down!

'But why?' Danniella was puzzled. 'Why would he do that?'

The spirits were upset because they felt the young couple were invading their property. And if things were bad now, they were only going to get worse in the future. We had to get them out and block the energy portal. It wasn't in the kitchen – where was it?

We moved from the kitchen down a hallway and into a bedroom. The energies were nasty there as well. 'My God!' I cried. Two children had perished here, two boys. That would also account for the negative energy and the psychic disturbances that had taken place.

Danniella suddenly put her hand to her neck. At the same time Melissa, who was standing next to her with her back to the window, tilted her head back, wriggled her shoulders and quickly moved to the other side of the room.

'Are you getting something?' I asked Danniella.

'A sharp pain down the back of my neck,' she said, putting her hand up to indicate the left side of her neck.

We both asked what Melissa had felt. 'A tickling,' she said.

It seemed the spirits hadn't wanted us to enter this room. This was where they had kept the children. They had been locked in. I could hear them screaming and shouting, but no one had come to help them and they had starved to death. Now, thanks to their traumatic passing, they were grounded spirits.

'I've now got pains down my ears,' said Danniella, putting her hands on her ears. 'What, have you got it as well?' She turned to Dane, who was standing on her left, where Melissa had been before.

'Yes,' he said, rubbing the right side of his neck.

This was the vortex, where the spirits were entering the atmosphere.

I felt that the man and woman knew what had happened
to the children – that they had been responsible for it.

'Do you think they've kidnapped these children?'
Danniella asked me.

'I do.'

'What, and just starved them and left them?'Danniella
couldn't believe it.

I knew we had to get these spirits out, to send them on
their way so that they wouldn't cause trouble here any
more.

'Davies!'I challenged.'Show us some of your evil!'

We all waited.

Melissa heard it first. It was a tapping on the window.

'Come on,'I started,'we've heard you've done so many
despicable things —'

I broke off as Melissa, who was standing once more with
her back to the window, was indicating that something was
happening outside.

'Someone's walking on that grass…'she said.

We all moved towards the window and I raised the sash.

'It sounded as though somebody was walking on the
grass,'Dane said to me,'but out there there's just a little tiny
ledge.'

I stuck my head out of the window to see if there was
anything out there and the next moment, to my surprise,
the spirit man had pushed me back and I was channelling

him. He was very strong and it felt as if he was holding me back. I have no recollection of what happened after that, but they told me that pandemonium broke out.

'He went absolutely crazy from there and just knocked me flying. My first reaction was to protect my girlfriend.'

Dane

Melissa screamed and ran. Danniella cried, 'Oh my God!' The spirit man was stamping and grunting incoherently in the middle of the room. Everyone drew breath and stared.

'I'll cut your throat!'

It wasn't a very polite introduction!

'Who are you?' Danniella asked.

'James!' the spirit shouted. He rocked back and forth. 'I can't breathe!'

'Why did you hurt the children?'

'I wanted to.'

'Why? They're not your children!'

'They're not *yours*!'

'Why are you here? Why are you bullying these —'

'Go away, slut!'

Of course this is not the way I would normally address Danniella! She knew, though, that it wasn't me speaking.

'I found that really, really hard to take. I was like, "Wow, I didn't expect that to happen," but I still got stuck in and was asking loads of questions because I wanted to find out about this man.'

Danniella

'When Derek's channelling, Danniella gets in there and enjoys getting the information out of the spirit. Angus is more spooked by it. He does it, but he's more hesitant.'

Natalie

'Why are you here?' Danniella shouted back. 'Why are you bullying these poor people? You don't live here, you don't belong here any more. You need to leave here.'

James sighed and pressed his left eye with his hand.

'What's wrong with you?' Danniella continued more

Channelling James – a stubborn man

quietly. 'You can't keep on harming these people that live here, these poor people.'

'Oh, can't I?'

The spirit man seemed stubborn but tired. He rocked and sighed and still pressed his left eye with his hand, as though it hurt. I had picked up earlier that he had been blind in one eye.

Danniella carried on telling him he had to leave, though he didn't seem that impressed. 'What's your wife's name?' she asked eventually. 'Because she likes to scare Melissa as well, doesn't she?'

James chuckled.

'What's your wife's name?' Danniella wasn't giving up.

'Anne!' he growled.

'Anne. Where is Anne? Why isn't Anne here?'

'She does things I ask!'

'Did she like harming the children? Was that Anne's idea or your idea?'

'She hates them! Hates them *more!*'

'No one's scared of you, you know.' Danniella looked as though her patience was wearing thin. 'I think it's time you went and let these two lovely people —'

James jumped up. 'I'm not going anywhere!'

Danniella stood her ground. 'You must go. You've got to go.' She laid her hand on his shoulder. 'You *will* go from here. You'll go tonight.'

James didn't think so. He lunged forward. At that
Danniella called for Ray, who came and laid me down and
brought me forward – not without some difficulty.

'I'm staying!' James cried. 'I'm staying!'

He fought like mad, but with Ray's help we eventually got
him out.

'Derek!' People were calling my name. 'Derek, it's Ray.
You're alright!'

'Derek, come on, darling,' said Danniella. 'Have a drink of
water now.'

I found myself lying on my back on the floor. I was very
thankful that the man had gone because while he was in my
auric field, although I wasn't aware of what was happening
or what he was saying, I was aware of what sort of soul he
was, and he was so alien to me.

It had been a horrible experience and I had to leave the

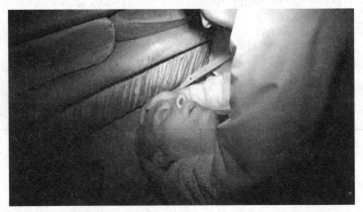

It was a struggle, but Ray brought me back

atmosphere for a few minutes to recover before we joined forces to send James and Anne on to their rightful place.

Spirit rescue

Helping grounded spirits to move on is known as 'spirit rescue'. In most cases a spirit asks to be released, though in this case we had to send James and Anne on their way. In any event, spirit helpers will come to collect the grounded spirits and take them to their spiritual home.

Back once again at the vortex, all four of us joined hands and I asked for envoys from the spirit realms to collect James and his wife.

But what a stubborn man! He was trying to come back in – without being invited! 'Don't let him in,' I said to Sam. But he was so strong he pushed me aside again.

'This guy James jumped back in again and channelled through Derek, and that was a really spooky experience. Dane was freaked out, I was freaked out and Derek was just somebody else...'

Danniella

'I'm not going! I'm not going!' bellowed James.

'James, you must step back, you must, you must,'

Danniella insisted.

'No, no, no, no, no!'

'No, you *must*!' Danniella was very firm.

'Anne!' he cried.

All this time I was struggling with him. He was a strong man and fought to keep control of my body.

'Derek, come forward. You must come forward now,' said Danniella.

Ray came and brought me forward once more.

'I'm sorry.' This was not proving as straightforward as I had hoped.

The parapsychologist's *view*

> **'It seemed quite unusual for channelling to be quite as violent as that, but again if the character that one's absorbed in or the spirit that's coming through is like that then it's not too surprising.'**
>
> Dr Simon Sherwood

We thought it might be easier if Dane and Melissa went and sat in the lounge.

> **'I was glad of that, to be honest. It was a bit much for me – and definitely a bit much for Melissa.'**
>
> Dane

Danniella closed the door and the two of us joined hands and started again. I asked for the two souls to be taken to their rightful home.

Still James wasn't going quietly! He was trying to enter my auric field again!

'James, step back!' I said firmly. 'Go and accept the justice that awaits you and your wife Anne!'

Then the tide turned – he was backing off at last.

'We've done it!'

I hugged Danniella. I felt absolutely drained, but so happy.

'That was so hard!' said Danniella. She later admitted that this investigation was the scariest in the whole of the first series. But I know her bravery and willingness to stand up to the disruptive spirit had helped these dark souls to move on to their true home. They wouldn't be troubling Dane and Melissa any more.

'I'll sleep a lot easier tonight and I'm sure you will as well,' said Dane, turning to Melissa, 'knowing that this has gone and that we're going to be OK.'

Melissa smiled shyly. 'I love Derek,' she whispered.

Dane laughed.

The very next day Dane and Melissa came back to the Ghost Truck to tell us that their flat was much better now.

'Maidstone's one of the only places in the country where the police have a file especially for paranormal experiences, so we had to take the Ghost Truck there.'

Natalie

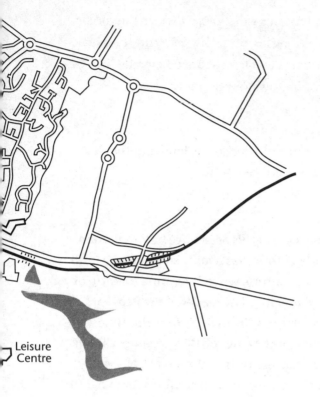

Leisure
Centre

Chapter Three

Maidstone

Maidstone in Kent is a cosmopolitan town in the garden of England. In its long history it has seen many turbulent events and it seemed that they had left their mark if even the police were filing away reports of paranormal experiences.

'My expectations of Maidstone, knowing that it's a very old town, were very high.'

Danniella

'People have lived in this area since before Roman times, but Maidstone was a fairly small village until the thirteenth century, when it became a centre of the weaving industry. The leader of the Peasants' Revolt, Wat Tyler, was born here. In Tudor times, the town also took part in the rebellion against Queen Mary and there were riots in the streets. Nowadays quite a few fifteenth-century buildings remain, but most are from the seventeenth and eighteenth centuries.'

Rupert Matthews, local historian

Profile Selection and Recruitment Agency

'I was really frightened before tonight, but I felt really at ease the whole time, so I was glad that I came in the end.'

Kerrie Marshall

This recruitment agency is on the first floor of a beautiful old building with a Tudor façade. There is no one above or below, but three members of staff, Cheryl Winter, Kerrie Marshall and Kelly Barber, came to tell us that they had often heard banging noises, mainly on the stairs, and had seen things moving out of the corner of their eye. A noticeboard had inexplicably swung from side to side, throwing off the papers attached to it, and the building had long had a reputation of being haunted.

As Angus and I entered the office I picked up the energies of a spirit man who had recently been there. He made me feel as though I was dragging my left leg. Sam told me his name was Francis. I wanted to go nearer to the energies he had left behind to see what sort of reaction we would get.

We moved into the stairwell and all stood in a circle and

joined hands. Though I didn't know it at the time, Cheryl had once seen a lady at the top of the stairwell looking at her. I opened the circle and asked one of the staff to call out to the man whose energies I had encountered.

'Is anyone there?' Kelly asked nervously.

Then something rather unusual happened. Instead of making contact with the spirit who had been in the building, I was becoming aware of the energy of a spirit woman who wanted to communicate with one of the girls present. She had had cancer and been connected to a Mary. She was showing me a letter 'S'. That was a connection to someone.

'My brother's called Scott,' said Cheryl, looking up at me.

Then a spirit gentleman arrived. Again he wasn't connected to the building but to Cheryl. He was telling her to hold her horses and stay put! Both of the spirits wanted to tell her that she should try to keep her feet on the ground

The circle at the top of the stairwell

more and not keep on making snap decisions. Cheryl recognized who they were and was amused. She bent her head and shook with laughter.

'Why are you giggling?' asked Angus, surprised.

'It sounds like somebody, it just sounds like them!' she laughed.

'When Derek gave me a personal reading, I wasn't surprised. I had been very strongly connected to the people that he was talking about and it was a joke within the family whether they would turn up tonight.'

Cheryl

As I was telling Cheryl that these spirits were with her, supporting her, and were very interested in her life, Angus suddenly said he felt cold air.

Soon everyone could feel it.

'Wow!' Angus was amazed. 'That's so strong!'

The parapsychologist's *view*

'That was interesting because there didn't seem to be any measurable change in temperature at the time that they were feeling that. Obviously because this took place in a stairwell in a multi-level building one

possibility might be that there were unusual kinds of air convection currents circulating around.'

Dr Simon Sherwood

This was a new spirit energy, not the people that were attached to Cheryl. I wondered whether it might be Francis making an effort to communicate now.

'Come, Francis,' I said, 'come forward now.'

The cool breezes seemed to intensify. They were swirling around us. One passed right across my face and Angus, standing opposite me, said he could really feel it on his leg.

'Oh, I don't like that at all,' he complained.

'It's not going to harm you, Angus,' I told him. This was just the spirit making contact, showing us he was there.

Then he seemed to try another way. 'Did you hear that?' asked Angus.

It was a faint sound, almost like something being dragged.

'Oh my goodness, I can hear footsteps or something,' said Angus.

'I felt quite frightened when I was in the recruitment agency. I hated those noises on the stairwell.'

Angus

Cheryl had heard tapping. Then there was a thump. It sounded as though it had come from the adjoining room, but we knew there was no one in there.

Next Cheryl turned to Angus. 'Did you hear that?' she asked.

'Yes,' he said. 'Like a breathing…'

'Yeah…'

Francis was certainly giving us a variety of noises. We waited to see what he was going to do next.

'My goodness,' Angus said slowly, 'that feels very strange.' He frowned in concentration. 'Derek, I'm feeling it a lot on my right hand. It feels as if I'm being tickled.'

'Well, OK. It's not hurting you, is it? That's good.' I was amused. Francis seemed a gentle, playful spirit. 'Can you do a bit more for Angus?' I asked him.

We waited and then Angus laughed. 'It's so tingly on my knuckles!' he exclaimed. He turned to Kerrie, who was holding his right hand. 'Can you feel this cold air here?'

Kerrie shook her head to indicate she couldn't feel the tickling, but said she could feel the cold air swirling around their hands.

'I could feel the cold air more on Angus and it was if it was where Angus and Cheryl were standing, as if it was behind them.

Kerrie

'Ooh,' laughed Angus. 'I can feel a wee tingle on my knuckles!'

I was so pleased that the spirit was communicating with

us in this delightful way. The feelings that were coming into the atmosphere were benign and playful. Francis was most definitely a very happy spirit.

We waited for a while longer and when it seemed that there was nothing more he had to add, I closed the circle. The girls smiled at one another.

> **'We're quite pleased we've found out more about Francis's personality. It explains a lot of things that have happened and will make a lot of stuff that happens quite fun really. I think we can interact with him more on a one-to-one basis without being worried when we're hearing things.'**
>
> Kelly

> **'We're really pleased that Derek's come along tonight and now we know who's been here.'**
>
> Kerrie

> **'It doesn't change the way we feel about the office, it's just that when we talk to him in future we can call him Francis!'**
>
> Cheryl

I expect that the girls will be having some interesting conversations whenever Francis pops in!

Maidstone Museum

'I'm a steward at Maidstone Museum. Once when I was in the library I got hit on the side of the face by something. I thought I'd left the door open and somebody had actually thrown it in, but I looked at the door and it was closed. There was no one else in the building with me, and I looked down at the ground and there was a penny, and I believe it was the thing that actually hit my face.

'I saw the figure of a woman on the balcony going from right to left and I can only describe her dress as "dirty net curtains". I have been wondering who it might be and it would be nice to find out.'

Peter Smith

Peter met Danniella and me at the museum, which is housed in a delightful old Elizabethan manor.

'The museum's a very old and very atmospheric place and after dark it takes on a whole new life of its own. Walking through it, there are statues and paintings with eyes that stare at you. You just feel as if something's about to jump out from behind a corner.'

Natalie

As we climbed the stairs, I felt energy all around me. By the time we reached a large room filled with pictures and beautiful furniture, I was able to say that it was the energy of a young lady. She was a spirited lady but there was sadness there too. She seemed to have something in her hand and was throwing it. I didn't know what the object was, but I felt she had already tried throwing it. She wasn't malicious, though. She just wanted to make a noise and to be heard.

All this time Peter was shaking his head in disbelief. Then Danniella told me about his experience with the penny.

As we stood there discussing it, I had the feeling that the lady was missing her father. She was looking for him, but couldn't find him. Sam told me she wanted us to be aware of her father Baxter. 'Is that a first or second name?' I asked him. He told me it was a surname.

I wondered whether the lady herself would come and communicate with us. I asked her to come past us, to come alongside Danniella, to let us feel her presence.

Even as I was speaking, Danniella said, 'There's a breeze coming right past me.'

'I was really sweating, but the whole of my back was really, really cold.'

Peter

Then we heard a noise up on the balcony of the room. We looked over towards it. Something was moving up there!

'Move towards us, please,' I encouraged. 'Come a bit closer. Show us your form.'

Spirit manifestation

Spirits can manifest in several ways. Sometimes a spirit who has just passed and is learning how the spirit world works may manifest as sparkly lights or orbs of light. These can be photographed with digital cameras and sometimes seen by the naked eye.

When spirits are more used to the ways of the spirit world, they can appear as a fuzzy outline or misty shape. This can also be residual energy, though. The floating white shape that people see as a ghost is far more likely to be residual energy than a spirit person in visitation.

'Did you see anything then?' I asked Danniella. 'That shadow there?'

We both pointed towards the balcony at once.

'Derek and I were standing on the gallery landing and looking across to the opening and it was pitch black — you couldn't see a hand in front of you.'

Danniella

'That shadow there, it's lighter than everything else,'
Danniella said excitedly.

'Can you see it again?'

'Yes!' Danniella was thrilled.

> **'The mist just came up from the right, went across to the left and back to the right.'**
>
> Danniella

I thanked the spirit lady. Then I felt her energies coming round behind me. She was showing me a particular scene. I was in open land and the young lady was dancing, whirling round with her arms in the air. Picking up on her energy, I started to demonstrate it to Danniella and Peter, who watched, fascinated.

> **'When Derek brought through the gypsy girl it was quite strange because one minute he was talking and he was quite normal about it, and then he said, "Danniella, I just want to dance!" His face lit up and he was beaming, he was radiant, he was happy.'**
>
> Danniella

It was a peculiar feeling – it felt as though I was wearing a skirt and dancing round.

'The whole *Ghost Towns* team was concentrating really hard. And then when Derek made contact with the gypsy girl and started dancing, the whole atmosphere lifted ... I don't think Peter had ever seen anything like it before in his life!'

Natalie

'It was quite fascinating to see the change in Derek. You know, he never ceases to amaze me ... That energy he had – it was great to see.'

Danniella

All around me I could sense a gypsy encampment – I was in the middle of a circle and I could hear the men, the music and the horses in the background. I could smell food – something being roasted. That was a first for me!

'Danniella, I just want to dance!'

Danniella was also amazed, but for a different reason. 'There's actually a famous painting in here of a gypsy girl,' she told me, 'which is maybe where that's coming from. Peter, is that close by? Would you like to take us through?'

As we moved off, psychic energies started pulling me forward very strongly. They drew me towards a certain wall, which was covered with pictures from the mid-nineteenth century.

Then I saw her – a dark-haired gypsy lady with her head tilted to one side and a garland of flowers around her neck, wearing a flimsy-looking off-the-shoulder blue-grey dress.

'This is her!' I cried.

'He actually went to the corner where the gypsy girl's picture was. That was amazing, that was really amazing.'

Peter

The local historian's *view*

'This was fascinating. There's a very famous painting in the museum of a young girl dancing at a gypsy camp. But what ties in nicely is that we also had the name of Baxter. Now the painting is by a man called Baxter.'

Rupert Matthews

'It's nice to know that there's something here that's trying to communicate with us, with the staff here. That's good, that's good.'

Peter

Doorstep **Divination**

'Clearly when we knocked on the door she was genuinely surprised and taken aback. The information that she received seemed to be quite meaningful and she seemed to gain quite a lot of benefit from it.'

Dr Simon Sherwood

On our way back to the Ghost Truck, I felt pulled towards a particular house. We stopped the car and knocked on the door.

A middle-aged woman with short auburn hair opened the door. Danniella told her who we were and that I would like to give her a reading.

In the Ghost Car on the way to doorstep divination

'A reading for what?' she asked a little suspiciously, as a dog
barked in the background.

'A spiritual guidance reading,' Danniella explained.

'Hang on a minute,' she laughed, disappearing behind the
door. Then she came back. 'Yeah, go on then.'

> **'When I saw Danniella at the door I was quite shocked
> and I thought it was just a wind up.'**
>
> Shelley Bax

We settled down in Shelley's comfortable living-room and
Danniella asked whether she'd ever had a reading before.

'No.'

'How d'you feel about it?'

'A bit sceptical.'

Shelley watched, somewhat defensively, as I began
talking. A spirit woman was there. She had been in the
house before, in visitation, and had heard recent
conversations about moving.

At that Shelley broke into a smile. 'I'm having my house
valued tomorrow!' she said.

> **'We've never had a doorstep divination where the
> person hasn't related to anything that has been said.
> Sometimes people have to go away and check up on
> details, or even find out things about their extended**

family, but nine times out of ten there's a positive response straightaway.'

Natalie

The spirit lady felt very maternal towards Shelley. She seemed to be her grandmother. She wanted her to know that she was going to stay close to her throughout this period of transition. I was getting a lot of personal information, but I didn't want to embarrass Shelley in any way. However, I wanted her to know that in her grandmother's opinion she was 'well rid'.

Shelley nodded in acknowledgement.

'My grandmother always let you know her opinions when she was alive. She used to say what she thought, so "well rid" was probably one of the things that she would say.'

Shelley

Giving a reading to Shelley

Her grandmother was also letting me know that there would be a new start for Shelley. She was flooding me with alcohol to the point where it was almost overwhelming. I had to tell her to back off a bit. Had there been someone in Shelley's life who liked drinking alcohol quite a bit?

Again she nodded quietly.

Her grandmother was saying she had tried so hard with that person but she was to take no more.

Shelley gave a rueful smile.

> **'It was very true to life, with the person that was drinking, with me moving and with moving on in my life.'**
>
> Shelley

I felt a little awkward giving such a personal reading in front of the cameras, but the message had to be passed on. And things were looking up for Shelley. A woman called Lynne was going to be invaluable to her over the coming weeks. Spirit works in this way, through the people who cross our paths daily.

> **'Lynne's just an acquaintance, but she's always been quite helpful to me in the past – and hopefully in the future!'**
>
> Shelley

I also mentioned that Shelley or someone in her family had a problem with their legs. Shelley agreed.

'I've had a problem with my leg for about three months – like a pain at the top of my thigh.'

Shelley

I was being told about a woman called Annie, too. Was she a family member?

'Sort of.'

I knew Shelley wasn't sure whether or not to trust her.

'No comment,' she said, diplomatically.

'Annie is my grandson Howie's mother. That was the only Annie I could think of at the time. She's part of my life.'

Shelley

She was definitely getting support from the spirit world, though, and might even have noticed something of their presence.

'When you've gone from this room into that room, just recently, haven't you felt a different temperature, that you're going from warm to cool?'

Shelley agreed. 'It's colder in there.'

That was because when the spirits were in visitation their

residual energy left a coolness in the air. Shelley looked rather surprised at this, but agreed she often felt a chill when she went into the other room.

'Who's been talking about changing a door with glass panelling?'

This turned out to be Shelley's back door. I went and touched it to make sure it was the one. It needed securing as soon as possible in order to keep Shelley safe.

'My back door – the lock's broken, so it doesn't lock.'

Shelley

Moving forward, I could see better times ahead. There was a dark-haired man in a dark boiler suit linked with the trade of plumbing. His name was Peter and he had a joyous way with him. He would treat Shelley well. I wasn't telling fortunes here – I was passing on messages from spirit. Peter would come into Shelley's life within a couple of years and all along her grandmother would be there, watching over her in her loving way. She might make herself known by a gentle tapping or just by a tingling as she brushed past Shelley – this was just to let her know that she wasn't alone.

'I did enjoy my first reading. Some of it was very true to my life. I could relate to a lot of it.'

Shelley

Feng Shui Chinese Restaurant

'We expected spirit activity at the Chinese restaurant because of the number of sightings that had been reported there, but we didn't expect Derek to give a personal reading.'

Natalie

Two brothers, Henry and Michael Lam, run a Chinese restaurant together, but they told the team at the Ghost Truck that they didn't just serve the people of Maidstone. Every morning they also laid fruit, biscuits, cakes, wine and Chinese food out for the spirits who visited their restaurant. They wondered whether the spirits wanted anything more from them and whether I could help them on to wherever they wanted to go.

'Michael and Henry Lam were very interesting to us because they told us that in their culture they have a deep respect for the spirits and they leave food out to honour them.'

Natalie

The restaurant was in a medieval building with a lot of character. The brothers greeted Angus, Danniella and me in the downstairs bar and led us upstairs to the main part of the restaurant, which was a long room with wooden beams running the length of the low ceiling. Standing there, I became aware of at least four spirits who came in regularly. There was a young woman who had lost her life in the building and also a little boy, though not from the same time. I could hear him playing.

Michael was nodding and I later found out that the restaurant staff had seen the shadow of a pregnant woman in the kitchen and regularly experienced a small boy running past at one or two in the morning.

Just then there was a thud from above our heads.

'What was that?' said Danniella.

'What is there upstairs?' asked Angus, pointing upwards.

'It's an attic, but I think it was a room before,' replied Michael.

'Is there anybody up there?' said Angus.

'No, only boxes,' Henry replied. 'We put all the junk up there.'

I explained that it was probably the child up there playing. He was just giving us evidence that he was there.

'My goodness, that was so loud,' Angus said.

Then the brothers explained about seeing the boy. I was being told that he had died of consumption in 1560.

The local historian's *view*

'At that time consumption was not an uncommon disease in this country – of course these days it's better known as TB – and only about seven years earlier the king had died of consumption when he was still a teenager. So it was something that affected children very badly in this country at that period of history.'

Rupert Matthews

Apart from the spirits connected to the building, the brothers' grandmother had also been there protecting them. Sam was saying very clearly, 'It's the father's mother.' She had seen them knocking their heads together over finances. The brothers admitted that they had been doing that recently. I was able to tell them that their grandmother was there to help give them the clarity of mind to make the right decisions.

'Do you feel as if your grandmother's looking over you?' asked Angus.

Henry said he did.

'I was really surprised when Derek mentioned my grandmum. She looked after me and my brother and we were always in very close touch with her. It made me feel very calm, very peaceful.'

Henry

I was also picking up that people had died in the building and that afterwards their bodies had been kept there for a short time, not in true coffins but in wooden boxes, before being transported elsewhere. That was in the fabric of the building, in the residual energy.

'Do you have a tunnel in this building?' Danniella asked.

The brothers nodded. 'In the basement.'

We decided to go down.

When we were at the opening which led to the tunnel I sensed a spirit person very close by, so close that I could hear them breathing. I thought it was a man. To see if we could communicate with him, Angus, Danniella and I joined hands while the brothers looked on.

> **'When Derek was doing his reading we felt comfortable. When he was connecting with the spirits, I felt calm and all the energy went to Derek. '**
>
> Michael

I asked the spirit to come close to us.

Angus and Danniella looked round at once. They had heard something behind them.

I asked the spirit again to come close to us three.

Again there was a noise from behind Angus and Danniella. They gasped and turned.

'Listen, listen,' I whispered.

It came again.

'Oh my God!' whispered Angus. He and Danniella wheeled right round and looked behind them.

'Can you do that again for us, please?' I asked. 'Give us that extra proof that you're here.'

'What's that all about?' asked Angus quietly.

'Can you hear it?' I whispered. 'See, it's stopped now.'

We stood still and waited. Angus closed his eyes in concentration.

After a while I said quietly to Danniella that the sound had seemed to me like the noise people often make when they are about to pass.

'A death rattle!' she agreed. 'That's what it was like.'

'Thanks for that,' said Angus.

I closed my eyes and we waited for a moment, then there came another noise from behind Angus. He cried out, 'Oh my —' and turned round.

'Listen. Shush,' I whispered.

'Oh, that's horrible,' Angus said softly. 'It's like scrabbling.'

We waited, but that seemed to be it. The spirits seemed to have stepped back. I thanked them for their efforts and closed down the circle.

The Ringlestone Inn

'The Ringlestone Inn, I was amazed by it from the first moment of walking through the door. There was just an amazing sense of oldness and quaintness, and it was the most beautiful place – the most beautiful pub I've ever been to.'

Danniella

Both customers and staff at the Ringlestone Inn had experienced paranormal activity. The young couple who ran the inn, Danny Holland and Jane Horder, told the Ghost Truck team they had both seen a woman there. Danny had been woken one morning by the feeling of someone sitting on the bed and had found an older woman sitting next to him. She had asked him if he was OK and, only half-awake, he had said yes and gone back to sleep again. Later he had realized that both keys to the room had been on the dresser and the door had been locked.

As Danniella, Angus and I approached the beautiful old inn, I started to feel unwell. Though I knew I was perfectly healthy, I actually felt that I was dying and couldn't do anything about it. I had a sense of foreboding.

We were met by Danny and Jane and all of us settled down

at a table in the bar. Picking up on the residual energy, I felt that this had been a place where people had been ill and had actually left their physical bodies. I wasn't sure when this had taken place but I knew they had mostly been men and I kept wanting to put my hands together in prayer. This showed me that they were a religious order – they were monks. I was confused, however, because when I asked Sam if this had been a monastery, he said no. I couldn't understand it. I said to him, 'Why a group of monks?' Then he gave me the impression that they were being tended to.

A little earlier I had been aware of energy coming round my shoulders, touching them, in order to test me. Now I sensed that a spirit was there, pushing my side. It was one of the monks wanting to step forward. Should we give him the opportunity?

Still sitting round the table, we all joined hands to conduct a séance. As I was opening the circle, however, the spirit tried to bypass things and enter my auric field straightaway. It was good that he was so keen, but he obviously didn't know how to go about it in the right way. I asked Sam to hold him back and help him to do it properly.

It wasn't very long afterwards that there was a second attempt, and between them, they managed it. Everyone watched as I frowned and drew a long lingering breath that was nearly a groan. They could see my lips move slightly, but no words came.

'It was quite unnerving at first.'

Danny

'It was a little bit alarming when Derek first started channelling, but within the group I felt very secure.'

Jane

'What's he saying, Angus?' Danniella asked.

Angus didn't know. 'What's happening, Derek?'

What was happening was that I was detached and standing to one side of my body, but because the monk had been in so much pain when he had been at the inn, through channelling him I could also feel his pain.

'She … left me … I died…' The words were almost incomprehensible because the voice was a groan. Then it got stronger. 'Maria, Maria, help… *Mariaaaaaa*…' It tailed off into desperate moaning.

'I don't like this,' whispered Danniella, turning to Angus.

'I don't,' he said. 'Too much pain.'

'The noises that he was making, they were just horrible.'

Angus

'I found that very uncomfortable. It troubled me a lot. When his head was literally rigid, right back, I thought,

> **"He's going to stop breathing in a minute, he's going to stop breathing," and it's not nice – it's not nice to watch.'**
>
> Danniella

'Derek, are you OK?' asked Danniella.

'Out, out, out,' I was saying.

Danniella had had enough – she asked Ray to come in. I was OK, though. It may have looked alarming, but I was fine. The spirit had left my auric field and I was aware of what had happened to him. He had been lying there ill and had called for a woman called Maria, but she hadn't come. He had been counting on her, but she had been tending others, and he had passed on at that moment. That was what had kept him there in the atmosphere.

The parapsychologist's *view*

> **'Because he didn't say very much, there isn't very much to go on, but I guess one possibility that perhaps Derek would put forward is that he was in some sort of altered state and this information that was coming through, this calling out, was some kind of deceased spirit. Another possibility, a more normal explanation, may be that it was another part of Derek's own personality that was coming through.'**
>
> Dr Simon Sherwood

I was aware that Maria herself was also there, though she hadn't stepped forward. She was a tender soul who had devoted her life to caring for the monks, and they had loved her dearly.

'When Derek picked up on the older lady it tied in with my own experience of meeting her upstairs in one of the locked rooms.'

Danny

'Has either of you investigated the history of the building?' Angus asked Danny and Jane.

Jane nodded. 'We know a fair bit about it, what it was originally.'

'What was that?' asked Danniella.

'A monks' hospice.'

'A *monks' hospice*!' Angus was stunned.

I nodded quietly. That explained a lot.

'The Pilgrim's Way isn't far from here,' Jane went on, 'where they would travel from Winchester to Canterbury, so this was a retreat where they would come if they were unwell.'

Angus and I looked at each other.

'For about seventy, seventy-five years it was a monks' hospice,' Jane concluded.

> **'When we did our initial research we found out that the place was actually built by the Church for the monks. Being so close to the Pilgrim's Way it was a natural resting-point for them, especially for the infirm.'**
>
> Danny

While everyone had been talking I had heard what sounded like a huge cracking sound behind me and now I turned round to have a look, but I couldn't see anything that could have caused it.

Then from around the same area we heard a kind of swish.

'Hello, the candles are going up,' said Danniella.

Behind us in the bar were several tables, each with a candle in the middle in a round glass holder. The flames of these candles were rising up, though there was no draught or breeze in the room.

'Look at our candle,' said Angus, turning to the one on our table, 'and then look at these ones here.'

All the other candle flames had started to bob up and down.

'If that's you, Maria,' I said, 'then make them bob a bit more.'

The middle candle in a row of four tables bobbed wildly.

'Wow, look at that!' said Angus.

'It's virtually jumping out of the thing,' I muttered.

'When the candles started flickering that was really spooky because it was as if the spirits were having a right old laugh at our expense.'

Angus

'Have you ever noticed that before?' Angus asked Jane.

She nodded. 'You can have one in the middle of a group and it'll go. Or the flames will get incredibly tall.'

'Look at that one go,' Danniella pointed. 'That one's going now, on the end. And that one over there!'

The candle flames were now becoming very elongated.

We looked at them in amazement. 'How odd,' Angus said.

Jane was smiling.

'The candle activity we've seen on numerous occasions, not only in this room but around the whole of the pub and the restaurant side, moving from table to table and candle to candle, either flickering violently or the flame elongating and becoming really tall.'

Danny

'Maria,' I said, 'if it's you that's causing the candle flames to be the way they are, please can you give us a continuance for a short time or do something else in combination with the flames, even to the table here.'

We waited for a short while. Then Jane blinked. She said shyly, 'Something's pushing me.'

'In your back or…?' asked Danniella.

Jane nodded. 'Mmm. Not hard, but enough to move me forwards…'

That was what I had felt before – a gentle push.

'Have you ever experienced that before?' Angus asked.

Jane thought for a moment. 'Not as obviously,' she said quietly. She smiled. 'It's still happening.'

'You're moving!' said Danniella, who was sitting on Jane's right.

She laughed.

'It doesn't feel uncomfortable?' I had to check.

'No.' She smiled again and seemed at ease with it.

I turned my attention back to Maria. 'Maria, if it's you who has just done that, gently again, can you do it again?'

'It's just a permanent pressure now,' said Jane.

'Is it?' I asked.

'I'm pushing against it. Not *hard*. Resting against it, I'd say, more than pushing against it.'

'Ooh,' breathed Angus, 'doesn't that freak you out?'

'No, really. Not at all. I'm amazed.' Jane looked quite serene in fact.

Maria was still showing her gentle and caring nature. I thanked her and the other spirits for their attendance, wished them well and closed the circle.

'Since Derek's been here and we've held the séance, it's been a nicer feeling knowing – and putting a name to – some of the people that have passed from here, especially the name of the person I've had the experience of meeting. So it's good – it's very good.'

Danny

To sum up Maidstone, as Angus said, 'There's a lot going on here. There's a lot of activity. I think we'll be back!'

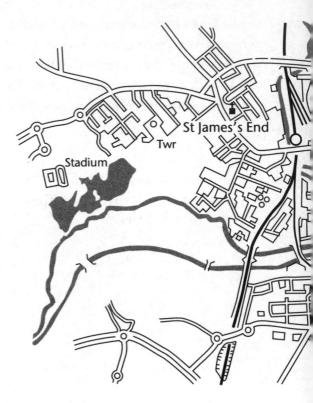

'I don't *think* I've had a paranormal experience,
I *know* I've had a paranormal experience in
Northampton.'

Angus

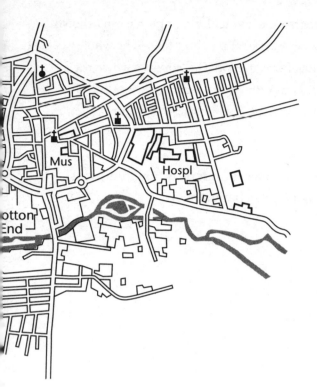

Chapter Four

Northampton

Though the programme about Northampton wasn't shown first, it was actually our very first ghost town. The whole team arrived full of anticipation. This county town in the heart of England was formerly known for its boot and shoe trade, but I felt sure we would uncover much more of its history…

> **'The investigations were underway. Anything, I just thought, *anything* can happen.'**
>
> Angus

The Haunted House

'Once Derek is here, he's so down-to-earth you forget that he's actually having a conversation with something totally different that you can't see or hear or have access to. But it felt really, really normal and I felt put at my ease, to be honest.'

Hayley Murton

Hayley Murton lived in a semi-detached house which had been in her family ever since her grandparents had lived there in the 1930s. They had brought up their 10 or 11 children there. Hayley had been there off and on since 1987, but she came to the Ghost Truck to tell us she was thinking of moving and felt she was being hindered by the spooky goings-on in the house.

Her brother, Peter, also told us about the strange activity that had taken place there. He had heard footsteps on the landing when no one was there and Hayley herself had taken numerous photos on the landing which showed orbs of light and other anomalies. Peter put it all down to his deceased aunts and uncles returning to their childhood home. Hayley thought it might have intensified because she wanted to leave. They asked us to investigate…

When Danniella and I arrived at the house, Hayley and Peter made us welcome and took us up to the landing. There were mixed vibrations there – many spirits had been passing in and out of a vortex which was between the bathroom doorway and the landing wall. There was no negativity around, though – these spirits were just coming in visitation.

I was getting a spirit lady who had had problems with her legs. There was also another woman. 'Does the name "Margaret" mean anything to you?' I asked Hayley.

After a short pause she said quietly, 'Yes.'

'Derek during the investigation spoke about Margaret, and that was our Auntie Margaret, who was married to Uncle Arthur, who used to live here as a child.'

Peter

Then I picked up the name 'John'. Hayley and Peter looked a little puzzled. 'Think back please,' I said. Very often during a reading names which don't mean anything initially are later found to be relevant.

I was also getting a dragging of feet in the landing area. Hayley looked thoughtful. Then Peter told me that he had heard footsteps on the landing.

'When I'm actually upstairs in the loo, I can hear footsteps stomping up and down on the landing and I feel that that is Granddad making his presence known. He's probably keeping guard, keeping an eye on the property. He wants us to know he's still here – that he's still in charge, probably.'

Peter

Meantime a spirit lady was telling me that she had been watching Hayley and was concerned because she wasn't eating properly.

Hayley had to smile. 'I'm a big Weetabix addict,' she confessed. 'I'll eat that three times a day!'

'Well, you're not getting all the things that you need, Hayley!' I laughed. Danniella smiled too and wagged a finger at her.

'I know, I have been really lazy,' Hayley said.

We were interrupted by Danniella, who had heard a groaning sound coming from behind her. Peter, who was on the other side of the landing, had heard it too. He called it a 'rumbling'.

I went to the place that Danniella had indicated – which turned out to be a toilet!

'I don't know what it was,' she said. 'It wasn't a pipe noise.'

As I went into the toilet I started hearing a voice. It seemed to be at a distance and I couldn't make out what it was saying. 'How do I pronounce that?' I asked. 'Is that a name?' Yes, Sam told me, it was.

'Do you understand?' I asked Hayley and Peter. 'It sounded like Mr … Mer … chant?'

'Murton,' said Hayley.

At the time I didn't know that this was their surname, but it was the name Sam was giving me. 'Mr Murton … and there would have been a chest condition?'

Now I had begun to feel it myself. Soon I was in pain and struggling to breathe properly. I started to sweat.

Danniella turned to Hayley. 'Did you have a family member with this condition?'

'Yes,' she replied.

'The man with the chest complaint that Derek picked up on while he was standing in the loo, we think he was our paternal grandfather, but we never actually met him because he died in the early sixties. But he did die of a heart attack and was always known by his surname. My nanna never used to call him by his first name of James, so it's really interesting that Derek picked up on a Mr, Mr "Merchant".'

Hayley

Meanwhile I was struggling. 'Take it off, Sam,' I said, 'take it off, back it off. Tell the man to step back.'

I wanted the pain to ease so that I could pass on information about the spirit man clearly. Finally he stepped back a little. He was a very regular visitor to the house and was a good soul, although stubborn.

'Sounds like Granddad,' said Peter.

'But was he the man of the house?' Danniella asked.

Both Peter and Hayley nodded. 'Yes, yes.'

'When Derek came to my house I was hoping he would pick up that it was relatives and that's exactly what happened tonight.'

Hayley

The spirit man was having a good laugh over something – he did have a sense of fun. I was also being shown a letter 'L',

'Who is the learner driver? Who wants to drive?'

'I can't say,' said Hayley, with a rather guilty air. 'It's a bit of a secret. My mum and my brother don't know about it.' She glanced briefly across at her brother. 'It is someone in the family.'

The parapsychologist's *view*

'Derek was able to present information that he couldn't have obtained via normal means. That might be paranormal, but in terms of what is paranormal about it, there are two possible explanations. He could have got the information from a living person, in other words perhaps Hayley or a member of the family, via extra-sensory perception, or I guess one other possibility is that he might have obtained the information from a deceased person, but for me, if we were going to put forward a possible paranormal explanation, the ESP one would be more plausible.'

Dr Simon Sherwood

The spirits were talking about Mary. 'Who's Mary?'

'Our mother,' said Peter.

It turned out she was actually in the house. She came upstairs and we were introduced. She was a pleasant lady with the same round features and blonde hair as Hayley. I explained to her that her spirit family had been giving me the impression that they'd been visiting her as well.

'Oh yes, definitely.'

'Who is William or Bill, please?'

'Oh, my husband is Bill.'

'He's been getting fed up because he doesn't know what to do with himself.'

Mary thought about this one for a moment. Then she nodded.

'Do you understand this?'

'Yes, it does make sense. Yes.'

'But there's good news linked with abroad coming to Bill.'

Mary agreed to look out for this.

'It's going to enrich your life,' I said meaningfully, looking past her to Hayley, who was standing behind her.

They both smiled. 'Thank you.'

Later I found out that after we'd been the spirit activity had stopped and Hayley felt so much better about her house now that she had decided to stay there after all.

The Grosvenor Shopping Centre

'I really hate it. I want to leave here.'

Angus

The Grosvenor Shopping Centre was built in the 1970s, but it stands on the site of a former monastery, one of the largest in England, and has long had a reputation for being haunted. Local psychic investigator Natalie Osborne-Thomason took Angus and me there to investigate.

Down in the basement of the shopping centre, in a corridor lined with grey breezeblocks, I picked up the energy of a monk who had left his physical life quite quickly. Sam was giving me his name very clearly: Thomas. I wasn't quite sure how he had died – it wasn't a natural death, but it hadn't been a murder or anything like that.

'I'm getting intestinal worms,' Natalie broke in. 'He was so full of intestinal worms he was actually vomiting them up before he died. And his stomach was all extended.'

She was very matter of fact about it. Angus blinked. This was his very first investigation and it was already providing rather too many gruesome details!

The monk was there listening to us now. He had been quite a shy character. I was explaining to Angus that he could come back here because the foundations of the monastery were still here when there was a sudden noise.

'Did you hear that?' I asked Natalie.

'Like a doorbell ringing or something!' she laughed. 'Ding dong! Let's walk down there – that's like an invitation, isn't it?'

We walked down the corridor towards the sound of the bell.

'It sounded like a doorbell,' said Natalie, 'but I don't think it was a doorbell.'

'No. Would you have doorbells here?' I asked.

'I don't think so.'

'You two can go first,' said Angus, falling in behind us and looking around nervously.

Just then we saw a bell push set into the wall.

'Let's see if this was it,' said Natalie.

She pressed it. No, that wasn't the sound.

Then Natalie had another idea. 'Maybe it was a bell, a handbell. Because the monks used to ring them when it was prayer time, didn't they?'

That sounded far more likely to me.

The parapsychologist's *view*

> 'You might have a brief kind of electrical surge or
> something, but what I think would be more likely,
> what I'd be more keen to rule out, would be a local
> noise. I'd like to have a look at what time this took
> place to see whether perhaps there was the local
> town hall clock or a church clock that might have
> chimed once off the hour.'

Dr Simon Sherwood

I spoke aloud to Thomas, thanking him for his efforts and
asking him to repeat the bell sound or to give us some other
evidence of his presence.

We waited for a moment, then Angus said, 'There's cool
air.'

'You can sometimes walk through a cold spot,' Natalie
explained, 'and you walk in and out of it – it's like walking
through a fridge.' Then she noticed a drain. She went over
to it. 'But the air might be coming up through here.'

It is always important in an investigation to rule out more
worldly sources of any phenomena in order to make sure
that what you are experiencing really is evidence of spiritual
activity.

Now Natalie was tapping the drain with her foot. 'It could
be cold air coming out of there.'

Angus bent down and put his hand out to feel around the area.

'Is it?' asked Natalie.

'No, it's not,' he said. 'There's no cold air at all.'

'Mmm, there's just a smell coming out of there.' Natalie and Angus both stepped back from the drain.

'We actually had sounds that were recorded and we actually felt phenomena, and quite quickly, so it seemed to go quite well.'

Natalie

The cold air didn't seem to be moving beyond the point where we were standing previously. Then Angus touched me on the shoulder. 'Derek, Derek, there it is. Here.' He indicated that it was now coming from over his right shoulder.

'It probably likes you!' exclaimed Natalie.

We both felt the air around Angus. It was true – the psychic breeze seemed to be moving with him.

'It likes you because you're a novice,' Natalie reasoned.

I could feel the cool air swirling around. It was a light psychic breeze.

'Don't you think it's a nice feeling?' Natalie asked.

'No, not at all.' Angus looked quite worried.

'That was my first experience of working with Derek
and I had seen other investigations where people had
felt cold air, but when it happened to me I was quite
taken aback.'

Angus

Then Natalie started to feel it too. We all put out our hands
and could feel it underneath them – swirling air that moved
from hot to cold and back again.

'My God!' Angus could hardly believe it. He backed away.

'I was freaked out. That continuous flow of cold air
around my hands unnerved me. Derek laughing
didn't help.'

Angus

'I can feel it on my fingers,' said Angus

Natalie encouraged him to put his hands out again. 'Tell it to do it again,' she said. 'Come on, we want a bit more. Come out to play…'

'Come on, Thomas,' I said.

'It's doing it, it's doing it,' said Angus. 'I can feel it on my fingers.'

The spirit was responding to us.

But Angus didn't like it. 'Sorry, I hate it.' He stepped back and dropped his hands.

'Do you want to move back? Let's move back out of the energy,' I suggested. 'OK?'

Angus nodded, but as we started to walk back the way we'd come, we realized the energy was moving along with him!

'It likes him!' Natalie was amused.

So was I. I put my hands out and felt the energy. 'It's to the front and back of you!' I laughed, delighted that we had such a result. 'It's covering you up!'

'Maybe it's never heard a Scottish accent!' Natalie suggested.

Whatever the reason, this was Angus's first experience of psychic phenomena and he was finding it difficult to cope with.

'I want to leave here,' he said.

We left.

'I wasn't so much scared as I was uncomfortable. I hated being down there. I felt trapped. And that cold air wouldn't go away.'

Angus

It had been an unnerving experience, but fortunately Angus was determined to soldier on! As he said, 'I'm out there with Derek and I feel that in a way he will protect me. I can't just stay in the Ghost Truck.' In fact I'm sure he's more than a little curious too ... Isn't everybody? I couldn't wait to move on to our next investigation.

Greyfriars Bus Station

'Then I knew I'd helped this young man, perhaps
stuck down this bus station for years. I knew I'd
helped him.'

Don Masters

Greyfriars bus station stands in the centre of Northampton
and has the distinction of being one of the top 12 buildings
in the country the public would like to see demolished,
according to the survey carried out by the Channel 4 series
Demolition. And that wasn't all – it was haunted as well…
Angus, Danniella and I were met at the bus station by Don

Angus and I leave on another investigation together

Masters, an amiable middle-aged man who had worked there as a night cleaner for five years.

As we stood on the concourse, at the foot of the escalators, I felt as though something was being draped in front of me. It was a leather apron. I was also getting links with a man who made boots and with the energy of a child.

'Is it a boy child or a girl child?' asked Danniella.

I felt it was a boy, around the age of seven or eight. His father was a shoemaker.

The local historian's *view*

> **'Certainly on that particular site there were houses that would in fact have housed shoe repairers.'**
>
> Gerald Smith

This boy had lost his life quickly, through something falling on him and crushing him. Because he had been so young and everything had happened so suddenly, when he had left his body he had got lost and not gone on to the spiritual realms. He had been wandering round here for hundreds of years.

'Sounds awful.' Angus was sympathetic.

During that time the boy had tried his best to show himself to people and get their attention. I felt that he had attached himself to Don in particular – he had come to see him as a father figure. His energy would swirl around him.

Had Don ever felt that?

'I've always sensed something about me,' he said. 'I have to be honest about that.'

'When Derek said to me, "This boy's been connected to you," that I'd been a father to him for some time, yes, I can understand that a bit, because from time to time I have felt as though someone's touched my shoulder or the top of my leg.'

Don

Later I found out why Don had come to the Ghost Truck: one night he had seen a glow of light on the concourse, by the escalator, and in it had been the face of a boy, in black and white, looking at him. It had drifted off towards the Grosvenor Shopping Centre doors and Don had had to pinch himself several times to convince himself he wasn't dreaming!

The boy liked being with Don, who was a kind-hearted man, but he was sad because he wanted to be reunited with his own family.

Then I got his name: James Culshaw. But his father would have called him Jim.

'Is there anything you can do, Derek, to help him move forwards?' asked Danniella.

'Absolutely!'

I knew I could help young Jim on his way at last. I asked everyone to gather round and join hands.

'You want to help him, don't you?' I asked Don.

'I do, yes,' he replied.

I asked spirit helpers to come and collect the boy, and very soon I was pleased to pick up on the energy of his mother, Rosemary. Then I was told that his father, Edward, was coming to collect him. He was by the stairwell.

'Which stairwell?' I asked. There were several in the vicinity.

Sam told me it was the one where Don had had an experience. I asked Don if that was right and which one it was.

'The stairwell just round the corner there.' Still holding hands in the circle, Don indicated with his head.

So that was where the boy was going to be collected.

I closed my eyes and listened as Sam started telling me more, but then all of a sudden Angus said, 'OK, hold on a minute. Right, am I going mad or am I going —'

'Why? What? Tell me, Angus.'

He looked confused. 'I've got cold air around our hands.'

'Don't panic – it's OK,' Danniella reassured him.

It was time to close the circle. We had done enough. Our request had been heard and the boy was on his way to rejoin his family at last.

As I finished closing the circle, Don said, 'Oh, I can feel something now.' He started chuckling.

We asked him what it was.

'It's like a trembling down my whole body.'

'When Derek sent him up into the spirit world, I felt my whole body judder – from my feet right up to my head.'

Don

'Do you feel quite emotional?' asked Danniella.

He shook his head. 'I'm OK, I'm OK.'

'I can feel your pulse – it's fast,' said Angus, who was holding Don's left hand.

'You know the feeling you get when you say that someone's just walked over your grave?' Don said.

That was Jim saying goodbye.

'I felt sort of a relief and a weight off my shoulders and now, afterwards, I feel much better, you know. It's as if I've done some good somewhere and I'm getting good back from it.'

Don

Snappy Snaps

'I'm certainly glad that the ghost decided to show itself and that we hadn't just been imagining things all these years.'

Janet Reedman

Snappy Snaps photographic shop is on the Market Square, one of the oldest parts of the town.

'We do see the properties before the lights go out and it's great to look at the buildings. I love old buildings, I love tradition, and I just love it when we get to the heart of the towns and see all the beautiful old architecture there.'

Angus

Janet Reedman had worked at Snappy Snaps for 13 years and had been told the building was haunted when she started. Most activity seemed to take place in the cellar, which also had a chamber running under the street.

'The atmosphere in the shop upstairs is as you would expect, but when you get down into the cellar part it

immediately becomes oppressive – very dark and very dank.'

Natalie

Down in the cellar with Janet, Danniella and Angus, I felt terrible. I was hot, then cold, and felt as if I was going to vomit. I knew what this was: there was a group of spirit energies down there, moving about. I could see these poor people dragging themselves around, bent over and crying out.

'Were they in pain?' Janet asked.

'Yes,' I told her. 'There was a group of them – it was a family. And they all suffered. And the last one to survive was the father, who was angry.'

I could see the man virtually crawling round the small dark space, screaming and crying and cursing God because his family had been taken from him. They had died here one by one, and their spirits had moved on, but this man's anger had kept his spirit here, and it was this that had caused the disturbances.

The local historian's *view*

'In 1675 there was a terrible fire here. Six hundred houses were destroyed. All Saints' church, which is next to the Market Square, was also destroyed. There

was no way out of the Market Square, so some families were trapped in cellars, and I have no doubt that the family that was observed by Derek was sadly trapped in the cellar in Snappy Snaps.'

Gerald Smith

As we were talking, I heard a rap from behind Janet.

'Did you hear that? At the back?' I asked.

Janet said that she had heard it.

'I've never heard that kind of noise down here before.'

Janet

'Who's here?' Angus asked. 'Is there anybody present?'

Danniella and I gasped. The rapping sound had come again. I pointed. 'Behind you.'

Angus turned.

'Can you talk to us please?' I asked the spirit. 'I can see your outline.'

'Who's here?' Angus asked again.

'Show your presence. Make a noise,' Danniella suggested.

We all turned towards where the energy was and waited. 'Keep talking,' I whispered to the others. I wanted to encourage the spirit to communicate with us.

'It's alright for you lot, I'm the one who's standing at the front,' Angus pointed out. 'You stand at the front.'

'What's the matter with you? Get out of the way.'

Danniella was quite happy to change places. She stood next to me while Janet and Angus waited behind.

'Is there a particular place down here where this has happened a lot?' Angus asked Janet.

She nodded. 'It comes in here,' she indicated to her left, 'and the door rattles.'

Now there were bumps and rattles in the area where I had seen the spirit's outline before. I explained to Angus that it was the spirit movement that was causing these noises.

He turned back towards that area. 'Tell us,' he said.

There was a rushing sound.

'Can you do that again?' I asked.

Then there was a tapping behind Janet.

'The highlight of the experience for me was when we asked if there was someone there and the ghost answered not once but twice. I've never heard the sounds there in the studio or in the chamber before and there was nothing else that could have caused them. That was really, really impressive.'

Janet

The spirit man was moving round the room, weighing us up.

Danniella was shaking. 'I'm freezing,' she said. 'I keep getting cold shivers.'

'Alternatively, I felt actually warm, almost sticky, while she was feeling cold.'

Janet

I began to smell something – a horrible smell, the smell of the rotting bodies. There had been five or six of them in a very enclosed space.

'Derek told me that the smell we had smelled previously, which had been like rotting fish, was actually a residue of the dead people rotting.'

Janet

The man was still moving around the room. Angus was listening carefully. 'What was that?'

'Then we started hearing sounds like crackling electrical noises, but there's not been any electricity down there for years and years.'

Janet

'Without a doubt there's movement,' said Danniella. Even as she spoke, there was a rap from behind her. 'It's always from this side, but we need something more than that.'

There was a thud.

'Thank you, that was great!' Danniella was delighted to get such a quick response.

Then there was a rushing noise and a shadow seemed to move above us. Everyone cried out at once. Danniella was curious, but Janet and Angus were unnerved.

'This place is horrible!' Angus complained.

'It's only just recently that we've even started daring to come in here,' Janet said, a little shakily.

'It wasn't so much that I *was* scared, it was just that horrible feeling of being in a basement, being encapsulated, being subterranean. It was dark, it was horrible, it was dingy.'

Angus

'I was a little bit scared as well, I must admit, down there. It was that warm clammy feeling ... I actually felt a little bit light-headed as well.'

Janet

'Janet, what do you think of what Derek's told us tonight?' Angus asked.

'I think that it's very interesting,' she replied. 'It certainly would tally a lot with the dreadful smells that we've had around the area and the general behaviour of the door shutting, and the knocking rather than materialization.

It does seem that he's unhappy, he's wandering through, but that he doesn't want help, that he doesn't want to be disturbed, basically.'

After we'd stopped filming, though, I did help this man to move onward to his spiritual home, where he could be reunited with his loved ones at long last.

The Wig and Pen
Public House

'His voice changed, his face contorted, and for me it was a really moving experience to watch. Quite scary.'

Danniella

Bar attendant Kate Lewis had come to the Ghost Truck to tell the team that all the girls working at the Wig and Pen in the town centre had experienced strange events. Many other people said the same, including a couple of regulars, Lisa Perry and Kathy Masters. Kathy said that glasses had moved of their own accord, the table had been shaken and she had felt a strange presence every time she had been in the pub.

Even before Danniella and I arrived at the pub I started to feel the psychic vibrations develop and build, and I thought, 'Whoah, something special's going to happen here.' Full of anticipation, I met the bar staff, and Lisa and Kathy, and we all settled round a table in the bar to conduct a séance.

'When we were sitting down at the table and we all had our hands around the table, we felt very clammy. It felt as if somebody was pushing down on our hands.'

Lisa

The first thing that happened was that a voice whispered in my ear, 'He belonged. He belonged here. He still belongs here.'

This spirit man was angry because things had changed in the pub, but I knew he had a sense of humour too, because he liked to fiddle about with the barrels down in the cellar. He was having a good laugh, saying that everyone thought he was a poltergeist, but he wasn't. He was a former landlord.

'Black Lion,' he was telling me, 'Black Lion.' I didn't know at the time, but that is another old Northampton pub, and reputedly also haunted.

Then I got his name: George Long.

I asked him to step forward. Sure enough, there was a slight tug on the table on which we were all resting our hands.

'Is this table moving?' asked Danniella. 'I'm feeling it, I'm really feeling it, but I just have to keep opening my eyes to look.'

'What surprised me most was when we had our hands down on the table and there was the pressing down and the table moving. That really surprised me, because I expected nothing to happen really.'

Lisa

'If that's you, George, please continue to do this,' I said.

Table turning and tilting

Table turning and table tilting were fashionable in the nineteenth century. With table turning, a group of people would stand or sit around a circular table, place their fingers on the edge and ask the spirits questions, asking them to reply by moving the table clockwise for 'yes' and anti-clockwise for 'no'. With table tilting, the process was the same, except that the spirits would tilt or tip the table up in one direction for 'yes' and another for 'no'.

Nowadays during a séance the presiding medium will sometimes ask any spirit present to make themselves known by tilting or moving the table. I have been present at table-tilting sessions where the spirit people have not only tilted the table but even moved it several feet around the room.

George continued to move the table. We all felt it judder and shake beneath our hands. I thanked him for his efforts.

'Considering these tables are solid wood, with metal on them, that was just unbelievable.'

Lisa

'Derek, do you think there's the possibility of us standing,' asked Danniella,'to make the energy stronger?'

'We could try,' I replied.'It could pay dividends.'

Holding hands now, so as to keep the circle of energy unbroken, we all rose to our feet.

I knew George was a very outgoing and flamboyant character, and I encouraged him to show his true nature. 'Come on, show us what you can do! So you're moving the table – do something else, George.'

At first he responded by moving the table once more. But then as we all stood there waiting, I felt the energy start to

'Are you in lots of pain?''Agony!'

build really quickly and I realized I was going to channel him. The next moment I was standing to one side. With a long sigh George began to communicate.

'Me leg, me leg, me leg, me leg, my leg,' he complained, in a gruff voice totally unlike my own.'Let me sit … down.'

Everyone looked on, still standing, as George sat down heavily, stretching his leg in front of him.

> **'Obviously Derek's got a great gift, but I think it's just amazing how somebody else can literally take over and through Derek express who they are, what they are, their personality.'**
>
> Danniella

'Are you in lots of pain?' Danniella asked.

'Agony!'

'What's wrong with you?'

'*My bloody leg*! Who are you?'

'I'm Danniella. I've been talking to you and asking you to show yourself and now you're here.'

> **'When Derek said that something strange was going to happen, that he could feel it, that Sam was telling him that something was going to happen, I didn't expect that – George to enter his body. At first I was looking, I was thinking, "Gosh, what's going on?"**

and then it sort of clicked in what was happening. And that was a bit scary.'

Lisa

George started rolling his head around. There was 'itchy stuff' in his hair. But Danniella was keen to get more information.

'George, did you die here at the pub?'

'Yes!'

'Was it to do with your leg or were you ill?'

'No.'

'Did someone kill you? Did you have an accident here?'

'I fell.'

'You fell? In the cellar?'

'Down!'

'Go down? In the cellar?' Danniella was confused.

But by now George was bent over, clutching his chest and groaning. 'The pain, oh the pain! Me chest, me chest, me chest, girl! Me heart! Oh, me pain, me pain. There is no one. No one helped me!'

'The main thing that sticks in my mind is the extent to which George took over Derek. I didn't quite expect that to happen.'

Kathy

'Are you old, George?' Danniella asked. 'How old are you?'

'Fifty-one years,' he gasped.

'Where's your wife?'

'I'm going to know, I'm going to know … where!' he exclaimed bitterly. 'I can never see her, she's never round when I want her.'

'What's your wife's name, George?' Lisa asked.

'Izzy.'

'Izzy?'

'*Isabel*!'

'George, you have to leave here,' Danniella continued. 'You're not meant to be here now.'

But George wasn't listening. Instead he began to sing. 'Lucy, Lucy!' It sounded as though he was drunk.

'Who's Lucy?' Danniella asked.

'My girl!' George chuckled.

'Is she your girlfriend?'

'Yes.' He grinned.

'Does Isabel know about it?'

'No.'

'And where is Lucy now?'

'She's in there.' He indicated with his head. 'She's in the back there.'

'She can't help you?'

'No. She's … *asleep*!'

'Is she drunk?'

'What d'you think?!'
'Oh, George,' said Danniella, sadly.

'I was quite concerned about Derek at one point, when George actually took him over. At first it was fine, he was quite gentle and quiet, but I did get quite concerned for him, because it was as though he was getting more aggressive.'

Kathy

The parapsychologist's *view*

'Derek seemed to be in a kind of dissociated state. Now one possibility may be that in the dissociated state this character that came through was actually part of Derek's character that we don't ordinarily see. Another possibility might be that perhaps this other, separate part of his brain was coming up with the information based on things that he already had in his mind. Another possibility, of course, is that he was actually channelling a spirit.'

Dr Simon Sherwood

All this time George had been bent over, his hands clutching his chest.

'Are you about to pass now?' Danniella asked him.

'Come and help me, help me,' he begged.

'I can't help you, George.'

'I can smell alcohol,' said Lisa.

**'There was a strong smell of whisky. That was *awful*,
absolutely awful. All of a sudden it just came in ...
Ugh. It just stank.'**

Lisa

'Have you been drinking whisky, George?' Danniella asked.
'Is whisky your drink?'

George laughed to himself, head down on the table. Then
he held out a hand. 'Come here, come here.'

'Who, me?' asked Lisa. She moved across to him.'

He took her hand and cradled it in both of his. 'Go and get
Lucy, will you?'

'Where is she?'

'She's in the back there. Go and get her right now.'

Lisa wasn't sure how to do this. 'How about if I call her and
say to come here to you?' she said. 'Lucy, Lucy! George
needs you!'

'She's asleep,' George mumbled. But he didn't seem one to
waste an opportunity. 'You're pretty, pretty, you,' he went on,
still holding Lisa's hand. 'Give us a kiss! Give me a kiss!'

She bent towards him, but Danniella broke in, 'No, don't.'
'No?' Lisa asked.

'I felt safe because I know everybody's around, I know Derek wouldn't harm you, but at the same time it's not really Derek, it's somebody else, you know, coming through. And that worried me...'

Danniella

'I think everyone had their different opinions. Danniella's opinion was he was an aggressive man, whereas my opinion was he was a very lonely man. He had a wife that had gone and left him, he had a girlfriend that couldn't give a damn about him and he just wanted to be loved.'

Lisa

'George, we're not from the same time as you,' Danniella explained. 'We're just trying to help you.'

This seemed to pass George by. 'Sit down, sit down, sit down,' he said to Lisa, pulling her down by the hand so that she was sitting beside him at the table. 'Lucy, Lucy, Lucy ...' he started singing again.

'We can't contact Lucy,' Danniella told him.

'Where's she gone?' George asked. Then he broke out into more drunken singing. This was more than enough! Ray came in. Still singing, George was led round the pub until I felt his presence leave me and I came back to myself.

I rested for a while and then Danniella asked me to come back and join the rest of the group to close the circle down.

I was aware that the man I had channelled hadn't been of altogether the highest character and I sincerely hoped he hadn't been offensive to anybody.

'I hope that whatever happened there, you were not hurt or affected in any way,' I said to the group.'Are you all OK?'

Everyone was.

I thanked George for his participation and closed the circle down.

'I've seen Derek go into trance before, but I just found that this particular time was a very, very powerful experience. I think for everybody present at the table it was quite moving to watch, and at times at little bit scary, but you always know someone's going to step in and bring him out of his trance, that it's fine, that he's never going to get to a point where it's worrying. But it was a powerful experience definitely this time in Northampton.'

Danniella

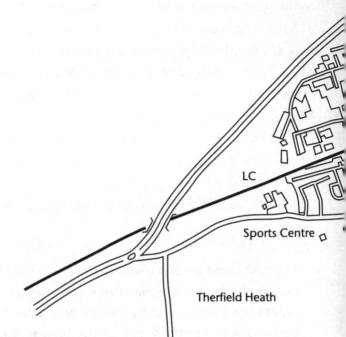

LC

Sports Centre

Therfield Heath

'Nothing could have prepared me for what happened.'

Angus

Chapter Five

Royston

Royston in Hertfordshire was founded by the Romans at the junction of two of their major roads. A lot has happened there since then and our investigations in this historic town certainly exceeded my expectations.

Banyers Hotel

'I think really the whole experience was quite enlightening.'

Diane Bathie

Banyers Hotel is an elegant former Georgian manor house in Royston. Diane Bathie and Delia O'Hara were convinced that it had at least one ghost. They told the *Ghost Towns* team that books had launched themselves from one side of the room to the other and that they had both felt an unseen presence in the hotel.

'We were interested when we heard about Banyers Hotel because it had such an intriguing history.'

Natalie

Danniella, Angus and I arrived at the hotel and were greeted by Diane and Delia. They led us down to the cellars where, apart from the usual bits and pieces stored away, there was an old tunnel.

> **'That was really a horrible place. It was dingy, it was like a dungeon. The floor — there wasn't even really a floor and it was so dark.'**
>
> Angus

We all sat down. I was full of expectations, because I could sense spirit energy to my left. I hadn't picked up on the person yet, but there was definite activity there.

'There's clicking,' said Danniella excitedly.

'Come in, come in.' I invited the spirit to come into our atmosphere.

For a while everything was quiet. We waited.

'What's that?' Angus suddenly cried out.

'What? What?' Danniella hadn't noticed anything.

'What did you hear?' I asked.

'It's that sort of "eee" noise,' said Diane, who was sitting on Angus's right, near the area where the clicking sound had come from.

> **'It was like a tapping on the panels, which was a bit eerie.'**
>
> Diane

In that area now, I could see a man in full regalia. He had appeared really quickly, which took me aback.

'He's a Roman soldier!' I cried. Then, 'My God! There's two of them! Come forward.'

Everyone stared, open mouthed, but apparently I was the only one to see anything. These spirits were just standing there looking at us. They were in visitation, they weren't grounded. They always came together, though, and they never left the cellar or went up into the rest of the hotel.

> **'Intriguing, what he said about the Roman soldiers. That was really fascinating – totally, totally unexpected.'**
>
> Diane

One of the soldiers said something, though it was indistinct. I couldn't catch it.

I was surprised to see the Roman soldiers

'Let's hear your footsteps,' I said. 'Walk forward.'

'D'you hear that?' Angus asked. He looked worried, but Diane turned to him, smiling and nodding. Angus pulled his coat round him as if he were cold and looked round the room nervously.

The soldiers were still standing back, though. They seemed to want to come so far and no further. I was about to address them again when everyone started talking at once. There had been another noise.

'It's close!' Danniella exclaimed.

> **'It was almost like somebody was walking on loose pebbles or something.'**
>
> Diane

Angus and Diane were pointing again towards the spot where the soldiers were standing.

'That's here, that's right here,' Danniella said.

> **'There was so much activity there. The noises, the repeated noises, they were crisp clear.'**
>
> Angus

> **'I've heard lots of noises, similar noises, all the time I've been here.'**
>
> Delia

Then a psychic breeze came past. Everyone felt it. I thanked
the spirits and asked them to keep on doing things for us.
In response, more psychic breezes swirled around us.

> **'The psychic breeze came from behind Angus, across
> the back of me and straight past the back of Diane as
> well. She felt it really strongly and jumped out of her
> skin.'**
>
> Danniella

Danniella asked Diane how she was feeling.
  'I'm fine actually,' she said. 'I can feel the cold air, but I
don't feel afraid.'

> **'I felt a shiver down my back and a distinct coldness
> around my arms.'**
>
> Diane

The parapsychologist's *view*

> **'There were psychic breezes reported. Unfortunately
> these didn't show up on the data-logging equipment
> — there were no obvious sudden temperature drops.
> Now this could mean that the psychic breezes were
> just subjective, in other words they weren't physical,
> or it could be that they occurred in an isolated spot**

and so weren't picked up by the equipment, or, because the equipment takes temperature readings at ten-second intervals, I suppose it's possible that a sudden psychic breeze might occur in between the measurements.'

Dr Simon Sherwood

Danniella wondered whether the spirits might respond if Diane spoke to them. I thought that was a good idea. They might respond to a woman's voice.

'Would you like to come forward?' she said, very politely. 'We'd like to know who you are. Come and give us a sign.'

We waited for a moment and then a clicking sound came from the same area as before.

'That's right by you,' Danniella said to Diane.

'Are we definitely OK here, Derek?' Angus was looking worried.

I reassured him that we were fine. We were protected. Nothing was going to harm us.

Then there was another click, followed by a moaning sound which seemed to come from above us.

'What's that?' Danniella asked.

'I'm not sure,' Diane replied.

Angus decided to address the spirits: 'You've been making lots of noises. Show us you're here in another way. Come, come towards us.'

We waited again. Then Danniella noticed something behind my head. 'They're moving,' she said.

'The cobwebs were moving. Wow, that was really weird. That was frightening.'

Angus

I could feel a breeze on my left side going across the back of my neck and down to the small of my back. Instead of moving towards us, though, the two soldiers were conferring, wondering what they should do. Another clicking sound came from the same area as before.

'Do you think that's where their portal is, Derek, where they come through?' asked Danniella. 'Because they don't seem to want to move far from that, do they?'

She was right – that was where the spirits were entering our atmosphere. But they could see the area as it used to be for them, not as it was now. That meant that they were in a field rather than a cellar, but they could see us there. That would be very strange for them. No wonder they were discussing what it meant and were reluctant to come forward.

'I can hear movement here,' Angus said, intrigued, pointing towards the place where the soldiers were standing.

Danniella had figured out what was happening: 'As you

said, Derek, that's where their portal is and they're not going to move from that. They're standing and they're looking and they're very unsure of what we're doing in what they see as their space. They're not comfortable with moving. They've probably never experienced anybody like us before, have they?'

I was sure they hadn't!

It was fascinating to see these Roman soldiers, but there was no need to do anything about them. They were just in visitation. They came and went. We left them where they were and moved on.

Walsh's Garage

'I had my doubts to start with. I was really concerned that we were going to be stirring up something we shouldn't be dabbling with, you know, but no, it was good, really good.'

Robin Binge

This garage and the house next to it stood a little way out of town. The people who worked there definitely thought it was haunted.

'Rob came to the Ghost Truck to tell us about the garage where he worked. He was too scared to stay there on his own at night, so we had to go there and investigate.'

Natalie

'It was right out in the country opposite a really spooky graveyard. It was in the middle of nowhere.'

Danniella

Danniella and I were welcomed by Rob, a friendly middle-aged man, and Gemma, a young girl, who both worked at the garage. While we were standing together in the workshop, I sensed a mixture of feelings. I asked Sam whether there was anyone who wanted to respond to us. Then I was shown what seemed to be an ancient fireplace. I asked if there was an unusual ornate fireplace anywhere on the property.

'Yes,' Gemma said.

It was in the house. We left the workshop and went over there. The fireplace was in a beautiful old room with ancient beams. It was huge and had horse brasses over it. This was the place I had been shown.

'God, this is very old, isn't it?' Danniella said.

Standing by the fireplace, I was picking up the energy of a spirit man. He was a hardworking man, a decent man. I could feel that he had had problems with his lungs. He was glad his chest was OK now.

When they heard that, Gemma and Rob turned to look at each other. 'My granddad died of lung cancer two years ago,' Gemma said.

The spirit man was trying his best to communicate and Sam was helping him. He would have had a problem with his knee.

'Yes,' said Gemma eagerly. 'My granddad had an operation on his knee.'

He wanted her to know that his legs were fine now. He was such a lovely soul. There was something about floors as well…

'Did the floors or flooring in a bedroom have to be changed?' I asked.

'In here, they did,' Gemma said, 'in this room.'

'Would your granddad have been part of it or would he have seen it from spirit?'

'He would have been part of it,' Gemma told us.

'Derek mentioned about the floor having to be replaced. My granddad was involved in that. When they restored the house, there was a problem with the water pipes underneath.'

Gemma Walsh

So far the details the man was giving were providing evidence of who he was, but my next question left Gemma confused.

'Did your grandfather shout at Frank?'

She shook her head. 'I don't know a Frank.'

'A little boy Frank?'

I suggested she ask her gran about that one, as that was the name I was being given.

> **'I spoke to my dad and the name that came through, Frank, from my granddad, we found out that his best mate from childhood was Frank Simmons.'**
>
> Gemma

The next message I was being given amused me. In his physical life, this man wouldn't have had any time for mediums!

'Yes, yes, that's exactly right,' Gemma said.

Apparently he hadn't believed the house was haunted either. 'When we said to him about the house,' she told us, 'he said, "It's an old house. It creaks."'

'Well, he knows different now!' Danniella laughed. We all smiled.

> **'I was really comforted by my granddad coming through. I didn't say anything about him before and the things that Derek said about him, to do with his chest and his leg, were spot on, so I was really comforted by that – that was really good.'**
>
> Gemma

This spirit was now going to serve as an angel of protection for this home, and I knew that he would watch over his family and keep them safe. But I was starting to tune into something else...

'Something was going on here many, many years ago. There was a group of children and they lost their lives all at the same time, but I don't feel that their physical remains are lying at rest in that graveyard.'

The children's plight really moved me. What had happened to them? Then I had it! I turned to Rob and Gemma.'Was there a well close to this site, or a place where there was a lot of water?'

'There has been a well on the site, but we're not quite sure where it is,' Rob said.

That was where the children had lost their lives.

Later I learned that Rob had called us in because he had heard ghostly'children's playground noise'in the workshop, sounds which then became frightened and panicky, and there was a story that a girl who had lived in the house had drowned in the well.

Danniella suggested going outside to find where it might have been.

The local historian's *view*

'In the local newspaper and coroner's reports there are reports of Ruth Mary Wilson, who drowned in 1886 in four inches of water, just outside the garages there, and also further up the A10 at Flint Hall Farm there was a young girl who drowned in a well.'

Ruth Stratton

It was dark outside and we had to be very careful where we were walking, but I was drawn unhesitatingly to a back area of the property. The well wasn't there, but it was very close by. It was the children themselves who had been drawing attention to it, because they wanted the truth to be known about how they died. They had drowned, five of them, all at once.

'Do you think that they could have been playing here, Derek, and fallen in?' Danniella asked.

That might have been it. I was definitely getting the impression that it had happened quickly. It was the shock that had left them unable to move on.

'Do you think the remains aren't in the graveyard because they were trapped in the well and the bodies are left there?' said Danniella.

Yes, I did. I also thought that it had been an accident rather than a deliberate act. The horror of a murder would have engulfed me. There was nothing like that in the residual energy here.

Now I was being drawn to a different part of the property. 'Can we go into that end there?' I asked.

'You go to where you need to be,' Danniella said.

We entered part of the workshop. It was time to help these poor souls to move on to their spiritual home. We all joined hands to link our energies together and I asked for the souls of the children to be collected.

Even as I was speaking there was a fluttering noise from above us. 'What the hell was that?' said Danniella. 'That was like running across the roof.'

'I don't know what went on on the roof. Not quite sure what that was — especially at this time of night!'

Rob

Whatever it was, it wasn't a problem. I continued asking for help for the children. Then I was told that the water where they had perished was only 30 yards away to the back.

'There's a sunken garden out there, an old sunken garden. It's well overgrown,' Rob informed me.

'When Derek pointed out where he thought the well was, that tied in with other stories.'

Rob

Now I was being told that the children would be collected. They would finally be at rest and the garage and house would be troubled no more.

For me personally, this visit to the garage was the highlight of our stay in Royston. The most important part of my work for spirit is to give help where help is needed, and I was so happy to think that these children had been released from this world at long last and reunited with their parents.

'If they weren't at rest, then I'm glad to think that they are now.'

Gemma

Doorstep Divination

'I don't know whether you believe in fate, but I do.
Tonight I needed this.'

Leah Francombe

On the way back to the Ghost Truck, I was drawn to a
particular house. It was time for a doorstep divination.

As we arrived, a man and his young daughter were already
on the doorstep, looking out to see who it was coming to
visit them. As Danniella explained why we were there,
another two children and a blonde woman appeared.

I pointed out the house for the doorstep divination

'Would you be happy for Derek to give you a reading?'
Danniella asked.

'Come in,' she said at once.

As we settled down in the living-room, I gave Leah the
first impressions I was receiving. There was a lot of love
there for her from a lady in the spirit world. At first I was just
aware of her, but it was only moments before she began to
communicate directly with me. She was Leah's mother's
mother. She also had Leah's aunt with her and wanted to
tell her that she was fine now.

At this Leah's eyes widened. She sat very still, watching
me intently.

One of the ladies was talking about Lillian. At that name,
Leah gasped.

'Does that mean something to you?' asked Danniella.
Leah nodded.

**'Lillian was my nan. I've always thought that my nan was
in the house with me. I can smell her – it's her perfume, a
smell that was hers. I don't know anybody else who uses
it or smelled like that, so I know she's here.'**

Leah

These spirits had been here today, listening to conversations
about Lillian. 'Would you understand this?' I asked.

Leah nodded again.

There was news coming to her from John. She wasn't expecting it, but it would be pleasurable.

'I don't know if it will be!' she said sceptically. But the message definitely meant something, as she was crying and laughing at the same time! Both Danniella and I reassured her, telling her that the news would surprise her, but that she wasn't to worry.

The spirits were now talking about Dave. 'Who's Dave?'

'Oh my God,' Leah cried, putting her hands up to her face.

'I am convinced that there's life after death and spirits and things like that, but I wasn't 100 per cent convinced because I've never had names given to me before.'

Leah

I wasn't sure how to put this. 'Can you have a good laugh with David? Do you understand that?'

Leah nodded.

'But not too many people are laughing around David, are they?'

Leah shook her head. 'No.'

Then I had another name: Christine. The spirits were trying to pick her up, to support her.

The names were coming thick and fast. 'They're giving me the name "Peter". What link is he to you?'

'My husband.'

'Well, your gran is giving him nine out of ten!'

Leah had to laugh.

'I know she liked him, but I don't think he'll ever be ten out of ten as far as my nan's concerned. I don't think she ever thought anybody would be good enough for me.'

Leah

'Leah's husband, Peter, was a total sceptic when it came to psychic readings, but he sat in the kitchen and when he heard what was going on he was overcome. It changed his views completely! Both of them later came to the live show in York.'

Natalie

The spirits had been listening in to family discussions about needing a bigger place. Leah laughed and nodded.

Now I was being shown two numbers: 1, 2. What did it mean? Leah's gran explained. Twelve years ago Leah had cried and hugged her and told her she didn't want her to go, but she had had to leave. As she was telling me this, her energy came so close to me that it was almost overwhelming. I had to ask her to step back. I drew a long breath. This lady had a deep love for her granddaughter.

'My nan died 12 years ago. Derek said to me that I asked her not to go and she said that she had to go sometime.'

Leah

Now she was placing a necklace round my neck.

'Is there a necklace that you were given?' I asked Leah.

'Not directly, no,' she replied. 'But there is one.'

'The necklace was a necklace that my nan had when I was very, very young. It was actually a locket on a very long chain, with a picture of me and my sister in it.'

Leah

'But you've got it? It belongs to you.'

Leah looked hesitant.

It gave me great pleasure that my message brought such comfort to Leah

There was also a ring.'Do you know of a ring of remembrance, a ring left for you, for you to wear?'I asked.

Now Leah shook her head.'Not that I know of,'she whispered.

I was convinced, though.'You have, you have. If it doesn't come to the fore now, it will filter through to you.'

Later Leah found out from her mother that both the necklace and the ring were supposed to have come down to her from her grandmother, but they hadn't been passed on. She has them both now.

I was being told that Leah's gran had been back to see her and that Leah had actually sensed it. She had been standing in the kitchen and her gran had touched her hair. Leah had felt it, but had wondered whether it was her imagination. I was able to tell her that it had been a gentle touch from spirit.

Leah smiled. As we finished the reading, I felt glad that I had been able to deliver a message that had meant so much to this special lady.

'Tonight I needed this. I know it might sound strange to some people, but I knew I needed it. I never in a million years expected somebody to knock on my door, but somebody must have known. I'm glad Derek's been.'

Leah

Henrick's Hairdressing

> 'The hair salon in Royston seemed to be riddled with ghosts. When they came to tell us about it there seemed to be a ghost in every single room, so we had to go and investigate.'

Natalie

Mark Henrick had been running his own hair salon in Royston for the past two years and during that time paranormal activity had been reported both in the salon itself and in the rooms upstairs. A mirror had flown off the wall and lights had flickered on and off for no apparent reason. Sometimes they wouldn't go off at all, even though the wiring had been installed fairly recently. On the top floor of the building people often had the sensation that they were being watched.

When Danniella and I arrived at the salon we were met by Mark and two young members of his staff, Becca and Becky. I realized that because we were surrounded by mirrors, this was an ideal opportunity to try some scrying.

Scrying

Scrying is a way to connect with people in the spirit world.
A reflective surface is used, either a bowl of water or a mirror
or a crystal ball. You sit comfortably in front of it and stare
deeply, but not fixedly, at your own reflection. After a few
moments your vision will blur and instead of your own face
you may see the face of a spirit person. The reflection of the
room you are sitting in may also change to that of a room
familiar to the spirit person you have made contact with.

'D'you want to take a seat? Let's get going, shall we?' said
Danniella enthusiastically.

We took the lights down and Danniella and Becky began
to stare into a mirror, Danniella standing and Becky sitting
down.

After a while Danniella said, 'My face looks different to me.'

**'I didn't expect to get anything and when it was me
I felt really privileged. I just couldn't believe it.'**

Danniella

I started to tell her that she might feel a sensation around
her face, but then she interrupted, saying, 'Oh, it's freaking
me out. It looks like I've got white stripes on my face.'

I could see it too. Another face was starting to superimpose itself over Danniella's. 'Just relax,' I said. 'That's good.'

'It's going down my neck now, Derek,' she said worriedly.

Standing next to her and looking into the mirror, I could feel it too. 'It's not going to do you any harm. Just relax. Stay relaxed, Danniella. Let it develop.'

'Oh my God!' she cried. 'I look like an old person!'

'When the transfiguration took place that absolutely blew me away.'

Danniella

An elderly man was superimposing his features over Danniella's.

'Good man,' I said. 'What's your name?' Thomas – it was Thomas.

'My vision's going in one eye,' said Danniella. 'In my right eye – it's going blurred.'

That was OK. I reassured her and she carried on staring, but a moment later she cried, 'It's freaking me out – I can see somebody different in there! He's dark-haired. It's like a hologram. Becky, can you feel anything at all?'

All this time Becky had been staring serenely into the mirror. 'I can feel tightness around my throat,' she replied quietly, 'as though I'm trying to say something but can't … Sometimes there was a smoky kind of look.'

I asked if Danniella was still feeling any sensation.

'It's going,' she replied. 'It's fading out. It was very, very strong and this eye was completely like having a cataract – it was blurred, completely blurred over.' She passed her hand over her right eye.

I was satisfied that the scrying had produced some evidence and thrilled that it had been experienced by people who didn't have any mediumship skills.

The parapsychologist's *view*

> 'Danniella could have entered a slightly altered state of consciousness, which we might call a hypnagogic state. This is the state that we're in just as we're falling asleep, between wakefulness and sleep. The thing about this state is that one can experience a variety of sensations and images. Danniella at one point mentioned she could see white stripes across her face. For me, that could be one possible explanation for what she saw in the mirror.'

Dr Simon Sherwood

We decided to go into the rooms above the salon. Mark led us up the stairs. At once I felt my lungs being affected. This was the energy of the spirit man again.

'Is there anything you'd like to do to get in touch with this guy?' Danniella asked.

We all stood together quietly in a circle and asked for a

connection with him. I asked Thomas to come close to me, but a couple of times I had to break off what I was saying to cough. I felt he was trying to make contact, then stepping back. It may have been that he had never tried it before and didn't know what to do.

Danniella asked if anyone else was feeling anything.

'I'm feeling a bit fuzzy – in front of my eyes,' said Becky. 'It went completely smoky again.'

'Which is something I had downstairs…' Danniella recalled.

When more than one person experiences the same physical condition – something that doesn't normally happen to them – that is confirmation that there is spiritual activity taking place.

'I can feel it around my throat, that's really prominent,' Becky went on.

'That's really pulling tightly?' Danniella asked.

Becky nodded.

Then I got the man's name: Thomas Amory. I was also being given a year: 1921. 'Is that the year he passed?' I asked Sam. No, it was the last year that he was here. This was something Mark could research later.

Danniella suggested that Mark or one of the girls try speaking to Thomas, as he might respond to them.

'Thomas Amory, are you there?' asked Mark. 'If you are, go through Derek.'

I didn't feel anything then, but Mark himself did. 'I'm

getting pins and needles in my foot now,' he said.

'Are you?' said Danniella. 'Which side would that be?'

'The right,' Mark told her. It's always important to give as many details as you can when reporting anything that could be indicative of spiritual presence.

Danniella started shaking her head. 'I've got a tickling on my cheek,' she said.

Now Mark had an itchy nose.

'Tickling, like someone's got a feather on you?' Danniella asked.

He nodded.

> **'I had a breeze on the right side of my body which was really quite cold. And considering that it's so hot in this shop at the moment, it was really strange.'**
>
> Mark

These sensations all showed there was a spirit person around, but he didn't seem able to make any further contact with us.

'I think he's unsure of how to do it,' said Danniella, 'and he was a lot better downstairs.'

We decided to close the circle down.

> **'Now we've found out a bit more and it makes us feel a bit more at ease about who we're around.'**
>
> Becca Crow

The Old Police Station

'I got the fright of my life.'

Angus

The old magistrates' court and police station in Royston had been the scene of paranormal activity for some time. This nineteenth-century building now housed offices, and two of the staff who worked there, Carole Smart and Adina Finch, came to the Ghost Truck to tell the team about some of the strange events they had experienced. The toilet door would slam by itself, a clock had jumped off the wall and a plant had launched itself from the mantelpiece and smashed on the floor. Once a policeman had brushed past Carole in the passageway. This wouldn't have been that unusual, only no policemen were there at the time and this one had no feet. At the end of the passageway he had just disappeared.

I didn't know anything about the history of the building, but as Angus and I arrived and walked up the stairs to the office on the first floor, I started to feel the presence of a spirit man. His energies made me feel dizzy and inebriated, and I thought I was going to stumble on the stairs. This man had been a heavy drinker and had found himself in trouble because of it.

We went into the office and Angus commented on how cold it was. This was also indicative of spirit activity.

I felt the man was coming back to the building because of some kind of dislike or unhappiness. Sam was telling me there was a holding place or cell linked with the building.

Carole nodded in confirmation.

'I was amazed that Derek picked up on the cells straightaway.'

Carole

'Can you get access to it?' I asked. 'Can we go there?' That was very important.

Carole led the way.

As we were leaving the room and walking back downstairs, Angus said, 'There's a strong smell like whisky.' That was what I had been aware of before.

The cells were very bare and spartan. As we entered them I felt that somehow there was a link with water, a trail of water. Later I learned that Carole had told the *Ghost Towns* team that on at least four occasions the taps had been turned on full overnight when no one had been there.

'This place is horrible!' said Angus.

Horrible or not, I felt the spirit man was very accustomed to being in these cells. That was one reason why he kept coming back. Another was that he wanted to draw attention to himself, to startle people. That would amuse him.

'That is really strong,' said Angus wonderingly. 'Can you smell it with me?'

'Yes,' I said. 'It's been all around you since the stairwell.'

'It's just like a really strong stench of whisky.'

'Well, he'd bring that with him.'

'Can we make contact with him, Derek?'

I started to ask the spirit man to make contact with us in some way. Then Sam told me his name: Jack. He added that he was around and was aware of our movements.

'It's cold right here,' Angus was saying, but then I heard Jack's voice. He was giving me his full name: Jack Green.

I knew he was a mischievous spirit who loved to make people jump, so I said to him, 'Jack, you love turning the taps on, or the water. Come on, do something with this machinery! Touch the sound man. Make his sound go funny.'

Carole smiled to herself as we waited in anticipation.

'Make his sound go funny,' I repeated.

Then, as if on cue, there was a fluttering sound from the radio mike, as though someone was drumming against it with their fingers. The lights on the sound equipment started flashing at the same time.

'Whoah! What's that?' Angus cried.

'He's twiddling with his gadgets!' I exclaimed. 'Well done, Jack!'

Then it happened again. And again. The sound man's face was a picture!

'I was standing with my back against the wall. I had nowhere to go, I was the furthest away from the door, and when it started to happen, it did freak me out.

Simon Edwards, sound engineer

'Simon is without a doubt the most sceptical person on the team and he was quite freaked out by it.'

Angus

'Rob the cameraman is quite open-minded and he has felt a few things during the course of the investigations, but Simon the sound engineer always looks for the logical explanation. Royston really shocked him. Afterwards we asked him how it could have happened and he couldn't think of any logical reason for it. He is very experienced, but in all his years he had never encountered anything like that before. In the investigations after that he seemed to be more excited, almost as if he was intrigued by the idea that things might happen. He was definitely more open to the possibility.'

Natalie

The parapsychologist's view

'It seemed that there was a problem with the radio mikes. Assuming it wasn't a coincidental technical fault of some description, I can't offer a good explanation for that at this time.'

Dr Simon Sherwood

'Jack, keep doing it for us, please,' I said.

But it was too much for Angus. 'I'm going near the door,' he said. 'I'm not standing up there!'

He moved to the other side of the room from the sound man and stood by the door, next to Adina.

'It's cold again there,' she said to him, indicating the doorway itself.

'Don't worry,' I told him. But then in a fit of mischief, I continued, 'Jack, can you do something else? Move from where you are right alongside Angus.'

'I can feel this cold air right here,' Angus said nervously.

That was because we were in the place where Jack came in and out. 'You can't get a drink over there,' I started saying to him, but then I was interrupted by a scream from Angus.

'*Aaargh!* I got pushed, I got pushed!' He shot across the room to stand behind me. 'In the cold, on my back! On my bum!'

'OK, OK,' I put a hand on his shoulder. 'Let me just check.'

I went over to the doorway and looked out.'You're alright, Jack!'

'I got pushed, just on my backside, right there!'Angus was outraged.'I'm out of here!'

'Well, he's only responding,'I explained patiently.'I asked him to do that.'

Angus wasn't impressed.'God, you're not safe in here, you're not safe near the door, you're not safe anywhere!'

'The psychic breezes were so strong, there was cold air behind me, and all of a sudden I was just pushed, pushed at the bottom of my back. It was as if that cold breeze just went through me.'

Angus

'I was glad he was standing by the door, not me.'

Adina

'How are you ladies?'

Carole and Adina were standing together near the doorway. They were fine, just very cold.

Standing in the doorway, I could feel very strong residual energy. Jack had definitely been there. Despite myself, I was quite amused by his antics. It was difficult not to laugh at the paranormal poking.

'Why is he mischievous, why is he angry?' asked Angus.

I felt he would work himself up into a state cursing someone. Then I got the name. 'Sergeant Williams!' I said. 'He absolutely hates Sergeant Williams.'

As I spoke I could feel Jack's energy coming behind me. For a moment I thought he was coming in. I encouraged him to do so, but then he stepped back.

Perhaps he was returning to the old police station because he wanted to have it out with Sergeant Williams. Then I was told that there were two of them! I wondered whether they were a father and son. They both seemed to have locked Jack up in the cells at different times.

> **'The policeman who I think had the house here was a very big sergeant, and that seemed to be who Derek was picking up on.'**
>
> Carole

The local historian's *view*

> **'I found on the 1881 census for the police station that there was a police sergeant called William Hemsden and he had a son called William Hemsden, who was his apprentice.'**
>
> Ruth Stratton

'Are you going to ask him to communicate with us here?' asked Angus.

'Yes.'

'I'm going by the door.' He moved across and stood in the doorway again. 'I know I was going by the door before, but at least I can get out. It's such a small space.'

I encouraged him to come back in and closed the door to seal the atmosphere. 'Be brave, don't be worried.' This was a great opportunity to ask the spirit more about himself.

'Jack, come close again to Angus,' I said.

Gathering his courage together, Angus asked, 'Would you like to communicate with us one more time?'

We waited, but there didn't seem to be any response.

Angus had heard something, though. He turned and opened the door. 'I just heard a scraping on the door.' He looked out. 'Did anyone scratch the door?'

Perhaps Jack had responded after all.

We decided to move out of the cell. I told Jack to go back to the world of spirit, get on with his life there and leave these ladies alone.

'We know now why the taps are being turned on. It makes sense now – it didn't make sense before. You wouldn't expect a sergeant to do that type of thing, but a drunk you would, or someone who was very angry.'

Carole

'I'm glad I don't work here anymore!'

Adina

'The old police station investigation at Royston was the scariest in the first series, but it was the highlight of the first series too. There's a real thrill about being scared. I hate it at the time, but I secretly love it – I love it afterwards.'

Angus

'I was completely open to everything and hoping for a really good time in Bedford and I wasn't let down at all.'

Danniella

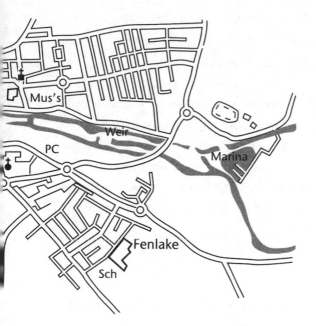

Chapter Six

Bedford

I didn't expect to be going to Bedford – especially as the hotel was in Stevenage. And apparently the team had a few difficulties getting there themselves.

> **'In Bedford we had some problems with the Ghost Truck – it was too big! We were meant to park on the High Street and the local authority said it would be fine, but when we arrived – on a busy Saturday morning – it wouldn't fit. Luckily the Swan Hotel let us use their car park – though they had to move all the cars first!'**
>
> Natalie

Once we were there, the doorstep divination didn't go quite to plan either. I was drawn to a house, but when we knocked on the door, no one answered. Then a woman appeared at the window. She was naked and had wrapped herself in one of the curtains! When she saw two cameras right in front of her she just couldn't believe it. It was obviously not a good moment for a reading. Danniella said, 'Sorry to bother you,' and we left in something of a hurry!

New York, New York
Nightclub

> 'The guy he was channelling, he really frightened me. He was one angry, angry spirit.'

Angus

The staff at one of the town's nightclubs called us in to investigate a variety of paranormal phenomena. Farrah Lawman and Amanda King told the *Ghost Towns* team that they had felt cold spots in the club, doors closing and other unexplained noises, and seen a mirror smash of its own accord and bottles fall off the bar by themselves. The club had even been struck by lightning not long before we arrived.

It certainly seemed as though the staff were spooked by what was going on.

> 'When we got to New York, New York nightclub we set up the equipment, but then we had to delay the start of filming because Amanda was so scared she had run off and hidden in an upstairs room. We had to send Farrah up to find her and talk her down.'

Natalie

When Angus and I arrived at the nightclub, I quickly became aware of a spirit man roaming the area, particularly the back of the club.

> **'I was very surprised when Derek took us to the back of the club. I didn't expect anything to be over in that area.'**
>
> Amanda

As we moved over to that area I started picking up the man's anger. It seemed that he showed this by bothering the staff. I wondered whether they had ever felt someone coming close to them or brushing past them.

'Some people have, yes,' Amanda said.

'And have they been alarmed by this?'

'Yes.'

The man had been doing it deliberately. In life he hadn't been very tolerant and he wasn't very attuned to young people, so he wasn't particularly at home in a nightclub. Unfortunately he was grounded there. It seemed that he had died on this spot – I wasn't sure when, but he had been in his fifties and I felt he had lost his life very suddenly, probably due to a heart attack. His name was Bill Henderson or Anderson.

'Where have most things happened?' Angus asked Amanda.

'It has been in this room,' she replied.

Now I was getting another name. 'Have you had a member of staff called either Lyn or Lyndsey?'

'Lyndsey, yeah,' Amanda said. 'She's one of my best friends.'

'She works here?' Angus asked.

'She used to.'

'Lyndsey used to work in the club here with me. It'd be about a year ago. She was a lovely girl.'

Amanda

Bill had liked Lyndsey. In fact he'd been quite attracted to her and had been asking where she was. The fact that she wasn't around any more made him angry.

'She comes in here every now and then,' said Amanda.

Not seeing Lyndsey on a regular basis would definitely have upset this man. He wasn't a tolerant person at all. Something as simple as the music being changed would also have made him angry.

'They did something to the DJ box the other day,' Amanda told us, 'to heighten the music.'

That wouldn't have gone down well with Bill. Then Sam told me something else. It seemed he had often showed his annoyance by making a nuisance of himself going behind members of staff and jolting them to make them drop things.

'What d'you make of that?' asked Angus.

'It happens a lot,' said Amanda.

'*It happens a lot?*'

'Yes. There was once … I had a case, and I had quite a good grip on it, and it just fell to the floor.'

'How? Why?' Angus was fascinated.

'I don't know.'

While they were talking I had wandered off to another part of the club.

Angus followed. 'Why are you moving over here, Derek?'

But I couldn't answer. Bill had come towards me, but then his energy had just dispersed. I had been standing there wondering what was happening when I had felt him come round behind me. All of a sudden I found myself rushing backwards and there he was! Angus was shocked when he saw me turn and growl at him in a voice completely different from my own.

'Who are you?' he gasped.

'*William*! Don't you hear me? Get out!'

Angus was so shocked he made a swift exit.

'This was the first time that I had encountered Derek channelling a quite aggressive spirit. By then I was more familiar with the channelling, but there are times when you just don't know what's going to happen and sometimes it's safest to stand well back – or to head for the door.'

Angus

The parapsychologist's *view*

'The most interesting thing about the nightclub channelling was the speed at which it took place and the way in which Derek's emotion and demeanour suddenly changed from how they were before, but he seemed to have no recollection of what went on afterwards.'

Dr Simon Sherwood

Farrah and Amanda were looking on in horror.

'When Derek started channelling it was very strange. I didn't expect it to be quite so in your face.'

Farrah

Farrah and Amanda were shocked when I channelled Bill

> **'It shocked me. It scared the life out of me. It was just out of the blue — he just walked down here and then started shouting. He seemed quite aggressive to me as well.'**
>
> Amanda

Bill just didn't want anyone around. 'All of you! Leave me alone!'

From a safe distance Angus asked, 'Why are you so angry?'

But it was no use – Bill just swore at him. 'Why d'you ask questions, questions?' he complained. 'Leave me be, leave me be.'

Angus persevered. 'We're not here to cause trouble, we just want to know —'

Bill turned on him with real venom. '*Get off, get off!* Are you imbecilic? You're making me angry.'

> **'The aggression and the shouting from the spirit coming through him, that really freaked me out. I'll never forget it.'**
>
> Angus

Then Bill seemed to find it hard to breathe. 'Bloody chest.'

At that point Ray came in and brought me back. When I channel such an angry spirit I can feel very drained afterwards. Fortunately, later on, after I had recovered, I did manage to move Bill on. It was high time he stopped causing trouble in a nightclub and went to his true home. I hope that he will find some peace in the spirit world.

The Swiss Garden

'It was a very significant and profound message that actually took me quite by surprise.'

Frazer Chapman

The Swiss Garden, at Old Warden, Beds., is a beautiful ornamental garden dating back to the nineteenth century. It wasn't long, however, before the *Ghost Towns* team learned that it had a spooky reputation. Numerous people had reported strange sights and sounds there. Frazer Chapman, an elderly gentleman who had managed the garden for four years, told the team that one day he had been leading a wedding party into the grotto and fernery when he had seen a woman dressed in the clothes of the 1850s. Thinking she was a member of the party, he had waved her forward, but she had dissolved in front of his eyes.

'When Frazer came to the Ghost Truck he told us that he'd seen a full manifestation in the Swiss Garden. Now full manifestations are really rare, so we had to investigate.'

Natalie

'How are you feeling, Derek?' Angus asked, as we followed Frazer along a path into the garden.

To be honest, I did feel slightly apprehensive.

'Arriving at the Swiss Garden made quite an impact on me because that was one dark and creepy place.'

Angus

As we approached a building, I was getting a first name: George.

'Frazer, does that mean anything to you?' Angus asked.

'It certainly does,' he said.

'Oh, tell us.'

'It's my father.'

'*It's your father*?' Angus was amazed.

'Mmm,' said Frazer. 'No reason for him to be here, of course.'

'There is,' I replied, 'because you're here.'

'When he came out with the name "George", it threw me for a while because George was the name of my now deceased father.'

Frazer

The parapsychologist's *view*

'"George" is quite a common name, so that alone is not particularly convincing evidence as far as I'm concerned.'

Dr Simon Sherwood

It may have been that Frazer's father was taking an interest in his son showing us around. I wondered whether towards the end of his physical life he would have had a reason to have clutched his chest, because that was what the spirit man was showing me now.

'Ah, he did,' said Frazer.

'Also quite interesting was the chest feeling, because he died of a heart attack.'

Frazer

'Was there a baby child lost in the family?'

'Yes.'

George had been met in the spirit world by this family member and had been very taken aback by it. He was giving me these details as confirmation of who he was. He also wanted me to pass on a message to his son, to tell him that the phase he was going through was soon going to pass. I felt Frazer was trying to make something happen but it wasn't happening yet.

'That's right,' he said, 'it's not falling into place.'

'I suppose for these past few months there has been a degree of waiting, waiting for things to fall into place, to move life, career, relationships onwards.'

Frazer

His father was just here to reassure him that things would work out.

'Good,' said Frazer, calmly.

'And sooner than you think!' That was his father's message.

I was also starting to pick up the presence of a group of souls. I could hear screeching and crying, as if they had been killed or perhaps incarcerated in the vicinity. They would be seen as shadowy figures crossing the garden.

'Frazer, you've had some experiences here,' said Angus. 'Can you relate to any of that?'

'This area is what you would call a hot spot within the garden,' he said, 'so there is quite a lot of activity here.'

There were certainly several spirit souls around the area.

'Are they happy spirit souls or unhappy?' Angus wanted to know.

I didn't feel that they were totally at rest. Then, just as I was saying that to Angus, they placed the vision of a tree in my mind.

'There's a very, very important special tree here in the grounds,' I said.

'There are several,' Frazer told me.

'One was used as a hanging tree – and it was used to mete out justice.'

This was what the spirit energies were coming back to. They were souls who had been strung up from it and hadn't recovered from the experience. They weren't actually grounded here, but they weren't at rest either.

'Well, Derek, there are one or two trees here,' said Angus, 'so if you perhaps want to move around…?'

We set off through the darkness, Frazer leading the way with a torch.

'These are quite significant trees. They are on the historic tree register. They predate the garden. Derek may be very right in his sense that one of them may have been used as a gallows tree.'

Frazer

After going past a couple of large trees, I felt psychic energies pulling me towards one particular tree. 'This is the one! This is it!'

> **'We actually did walk round to what was the historic entrance to the park where there is a very ancient oak and Derek did get feelings from that particular oak.'**

Frazer

Frazer shone his torch upon it.

'That first layer of branches in there,' I pointed, 'that's most definitely where they would have been strung from.'

They had been uniformed men – deserters who had been hanged for refusing to fight.

The local historian's *view*

> **'It's almost certain that there would have been a gallows somewhere in this area, and on a compulsory muster people would have to have turned up to join the army, and a lot of people would not have wanted to and if they had tried to flee they would have been classed as deserters and it is likely that they would have been captured and executed.'**

Bill King

'And are they still here in spirit?' Angus asked.

**'I must say when we were under the hanging tree, the
things going on inside my head – the idea of people
being hung from that big branch, perhaps
murdered...'**

Angus

Their energies didn't seem to have moved on, but I felt
that they wouldn't be showing themselves to people in
the grounds, rather making noises or appearing as figures
glimpsed out of the corner of the eye.

Frazer explained that just behind us was another hot spot
where people had been seen just standing and watching.
There didn't seem to be any malice about them, they were
just looking. That tied in with what I felt – that there wasn't
any evil intent with these spirits, it was just that they hadn't
really moved forward.

As we were standing there talking, there was a cracking
sound, almost like the branch of a tree breaking off.

'Did you hear that?' asked Angus. 'That was a loud noise.'

I asked the spirits who had lost their lives at the tree to
step forward.

We stood and listened. There seemed to be a lot of strange
noises around. The trees were rustling and sighing.

'What's that?' cried Angus in alarm. 'What the hell is that?'

It was a grunting sound.

'Ah, that's horrible,' Angus breathed.

'Just the combination of darkness and those inexplicable noises – it was almost too much. It sent such a shiver down my spine.'

Angus

The grunting may or may not have been a spirit, but they were definitely still around.

'Is there anything we can do for these spirits, Derek?' Angus asked.

Yes, we could help them. They weren't grounded, but they still hadn't overcome the way in which they had left their physical life. Frazer, Angus and I joined together in a circle to send them onward.

As I was speaking to the spirits, we could hear noises around us. Then I heard the distinct sound of footsteps behind me. I was standing in front of a fence. I turned and peered through the railings, but it was impossible to see anything in the darkness.

Sometimes when spirit people receive an offer to move on, they don't know how to react. I imagined this group had never encountered anything like this before and were gathering together and discussing it among themselves, wondering what to do.

Then Sam gave me an idea. Angus, Frazer and I envisaged a pathway of light, a path that would lead these lost souls home to their loved ones. Finally they were able to leave the garden and go into the light.

> **'I just found it very, very good to have Derek working in the garden. It was a very interesting experience.'**
>
> Frazer

The King's Arms

'The story about the rings at the King's Arms really, really enchanted me because it was quite fairytale-like.'

Danniella

It was a strange story that drew us to this beautiful old inn. Although there had been a range of paranormal events there, one in particular had intrigued Sean O'Donnell and Amanda Fitzgerald, who ran the inn. They had had a friend staying with them who had two children and when she had woken up in the morning she had found rings beside her bed and beside the children's bed. They hadn't been there when she went to sleep. Sean and Amanda wondered where they had come from. They asked me to perform psychometry on them.

Psychometry

Psychometry is where a medium picks up residual energy from objects. I have done it from time to time over the years and picked up some interesting information. Jewellery, furniture and paintings are the best objects to work with. It's always good to use personal objects, as they can give information about their owners.

At the inn Danniella and I were taken upstairs to a smart bedroom with pine furniture.

'And this is where the rings were found?' Danniella said.

'Yes. On the dressing table over there,' Amanda said. She passed the rings to me.

There were three of them, but as I took them in my hands, two of them seemed to stick together. I had to separate them out. It almost seemed as though they were interlinked, but they weren't. The other ring stayed separate. I knew at once what this meant. This particular ring had a double line of stones which looked like diamonds and sapphires. Of the other two, one was made up of different strands of gold and the other had a cluster of stones with a red stone, perhaps a ruby, in the middle.

'That's small, isn't it?' Danniella said, looking over my shoulder at the rings.

'Can I just explain that the two children's rings were actually found in the kids' room next door,' Amanda said.

> **'When Derek took the rings, I found it quite interesting to get the readings, and it was interesting that he actually separated them because they were found in two different places.'**
>
> Amanda

As I held the rings I was getting two different images. One was of a spirit woman and the other was of physical hands placing the rings.

'This is not to disappoint you,' I said, holding the cluster ring and the gold one, 'but these two rings here are not apported rings from spirit. They would have been placed wherever they were found by a physical hand. They were certainly placed for you to find.'

Apports

Items that are brought by the spirit world are known as 'apports'. Spirit people will find an article, especially a piece of jewellery, and will try and get that piece of jewellery to a loved one.

Amanda listened carefully and nodded.

'Have you children?'

'Yes.'

Then I knew that these two rings had been found separately in the public house. People had lost them and a little girl had picked them up.

I turned my attention to the other ring. I held it up. The spirit woman who had brought it had come back because of emotional ties. She was from Amanda's side of the family.

'Is there a lady who suffered some kind of body weight loss prior to her passing?' I asked.

Amanda looked thoughtful. 'Possibly my grandmother, but I'm not sure.'

'Derek, can I ask you a question?' said Danniella. 'Is this coming from the ring?'

'Yes.'

'I wasn't even aware that a spirit could come through and give you an object.'

Danniella

The ring was linking me to a spirit lady in visitation. I knew emotions were running very deeply here. Generally when spirit people come with one solitary ring, it's to help a person through a time of emotional stress.

'Have you felt yourself under a bit of pressure?' I asked Amanda.

'Possibly, yeah,' she said, with a rueful smile. 'As a family, I suppose, yeah.'

The ring was to give them strength and to show that the spirit lady was supporting them through this particular time.

'We've moved into the pub from another place and we're staying here for a short period of time and then moving on, so that did make perfect sense about the ring that was given.'

Amanda

The parapsychologist's *view*

'Objects that appear not through normal physical means are called "apports". As a parapsychologist, I would need to rule out normal explanations, for example that they were moved by normal physical means or by humans. If I could do that, then I would entertain the possibility that they could be paranormal.'

Dr Simon Sherwood

There was also spirit movement around the inn. 'I want to go down away from here,' I said. I wondered whether there was a cellar.

Elaine, who worked at the inn, nodded at once. 'When you're in there you feel sometimes there's someone behind you.'

'That's Jim!' I said. He was a person who had had a connection with the inn. He didn't come upstairs, though.

'Would it be easier for you to go downstairs?' asked Danniella.

Back in the bar, Amanda said to me, 'Derek, I've always noticed the plaque on the post – that's Jim's post. I don't know how long it's been there.'

'Have you just noticed that?' asked Danniella.

'No, I've noticed it for quite a long time,' she told her.

Sean and I went over and looked at it. The small plaque had the inscription: 'Jim's post. Remembered by all his friends. Died 26.6.81.'

I was pleased to get this confirmation. 'This is Jim's place, 'I said. 'Can we go down the cellar?'

Somehow we always seem to find ourselves in cellars. This one, where drinks were stored, was where Jim was coming in and out. He wasn't grounded, but he often popped back to the inn for a visit. He knew the place very well and was pleased to be there. His energies felt good.

'The kids talk about a friendly ghost,' said Sean.

That would be him.

'Jim was twenty years before my time, but hopefully he's happy with what we're doing.'

Sean

The parapsychologist's *view*

> 'It's quite a common name. It's interesting, though, that there is a brass plate on the post in the bar that has the name "Jim" on it – but again that could be just a coincidence.'

Dr Simon Sherwood

But what was really intriguing me about the inn was not Jim, but the spirit lady who had brought the ring. I asked to hold it again. This lady was resolute. She had come from the spirit world to see the family through this particular period and she wasn't going back until it was over.

Amanda listened carefully and nodded.

'You will start to sense her,' I said, 'without a medium being present. Just send a thought out to her, OK?'

She smiled.

> 'I'm just pleased to get the reading and I feel comfortable in the pub, always have done.'

Amanda

Twinwood Airfield

'I think the fact that Derek's been here has stirred something, something more than normal.'

Alice Wooding

A former airfield, Twinwood in Bedfordshire, is the last place where the famous bandleader Glenn Miller was seen alive. Towards the end of the Second World War he set off on a flight to Paris, never to be seen again. The airfield is now the site of the Glenn Miller Museum. The *Ghost Towns* team were intrigued by it because paranormal activity had been reported in most of the buildings. Alice Wooding, who worked there, explained that there had been a lot of strange electrical activity and a ball of light had once flown around one of the huts. Footsteps had regularly been heard in the middle of the night and an elderly man in a wartime RAF uniform had been seen by several people.

'The whole team was very excited about investigating there.'

Natalie

The airfield was way out in the country and I had no idea where I was going. Angus and Danniella did, but even they didn't seem to like it very much!

Setting off in the Ghost Car...

'It was as if we were driving into the middle of nowhere. It was pitch black – you could see the stars so clearly. I felt as if I'd travelled to another universe.'

Angus

'All of a sudden there were loads of these great big places that were camouflaged and spooky and everything. It was like being in the war. It was horrible.'

Danniella

Alice met us at the airfield and led us to the control tower.

> **'When we went up into the control tower there were a lot of very strange noises and the whole team was beginning to feel a little bit edgy.'**
>
> Natalie

Very quickly I began to pick up psychic energies. They seemed to be all over the place! There was movement there – I was sure that items had been moved around. It wasn't a poltergeist, but a playfulness on the part of a man who had once been in charge there. He had sometimes lacked a little bit of tolerance and could blow his top. I felt we might have a better chance of getting a response from him if one of the ladies spoke to him.

'OK, if you're listening,' said Alice, looking around her with a rather amused smile, 'please would you do what you do many times. You know what you do.'

> **'When Derek first arrived, initially I was quite sceptical.'**
>
> Alice

We waited expectantly. Nothing happened.

'Can we hear your footsteps walk along the passageway, 'I asked, 'if you don't want to come into this room? I know

you were impeccable. I know you were a perfectionist.
Please, sir.'

'Did you hear that?' Angus pointed to a corner of the room.

'A little click, yeah.'

Sam was giving me the surname 'Collins'.

'Possibly Wing Commander Collins,' Alice said.

'That's him!'

The local historian's *view*

'The records indicate there was a Wing Commander Collins who took off from RAF Lyneham in 1943 and actually crashed in the local area.'

Bill King

'Is he coming through, Derek?' asked Danniella. 'Is he trying to channel?'

I think he was trying, but he was making me feel ill. 'Take it back, Sam,' I said, holding my head, 'take him back.'

I asked if I could sit down. My head felt as if it was pounding and the front of my stomach was hurting very badly. These were the conditions this man had suffered before leaving his physical body. I was feeling his pain because he had not rid himself of the memory of it.

April 24th – there was something important about that date.

'What year was that?' asked Alice quietly.

'1942,' I whispered. Then I repeated it more loudly '1942.'

'Is that relevant to you, Alice?' asked Danniella.

'The airfield would have been very active in that year,' she said.

The local historian's *view*

'At that time a Blenheim bomber took off from the airfield and crashed locally, so that is certainly a relevant date.'

Bill King

'He can't stop the blood,' I sighed.

This got Danniella thinking. 'So if they'd been hurt in combat, would they have been brought back here and looked after, would they have been hospitalized?' she asked Alice.

'No, look,' I said, 'he didn't lose his life here.'

I felt sorry for him. This man put himself through torment to come back here but it was so important for him to come that he did it.

Then we heard noises. I couldn't make out whether they were from the corridor or the same corner as before.

'They're from the same place as before,' Danniella told me, 'from that back room there.'

We decided to go there and see what we could find.

To get there we had to walk down a corridor. All the doors were olive green and there was a very military feel to the place. There were posters and photographs on every wall.

'You can really feel the temperature drop,' Alice said as we walked along.

The room in question turned out to be a massive aircraft hanger. The atmosphere hit me at once! 'This is a really active place!' I exclaimed.

'Wow, it's cold in here,' Danniella said. 'It's *freezing* in here.'

'When we walked into the huge aircraft hanger where all the old dances were held, literally as we stepped over the threshold, the temperature just dropped to sub-zero.'

Danniella

'Can you feel the temperature drop?' I asked.

'From that room to this room,' she replied, '*massively.*'

The parapsychologist's *view*

'I set up a data log in the stage area. The rate of change of the temperature drop in the period we were in there is much greater than the periods before and after, when we were not. I would have expected the temperature to *increase* given the people being in

there, or at least the rate of change to be less. I don't think that alone indicates that it's paranormal. I would want to take another baseline reading and see if I got the same results when there was no one in the room.'

Dr Simon Sherwood

We all started to walk round the room, our footsteps echoing in the empty space.

I was picking up on music, talking, laughter. All this was in the residual energy. It was a magical atmosphere, really lovely. But I was also drawn to the stage which was at one end of the room. There was a man there, an important man, someone who had once held high office. He was a proud man, but a good soul.

Angus shivered. 'It's freezing in here, isn't it?'

'It's because we're being listened to,' I explained.

'He said there were a lot of spirits in there and I just felt as if we were the only ones in there.'

Angus

Then there was a thud from near the stage.

'D'you hear that?' I asked.

We moved towards that area. I was being drawn up on to the stage. When we were all up there, I picked up a name: Robert Jones. And there was a commander there too.

'*What's that?*' Angus cried suddenly.

It had been a muffled thud.

'Was that you, commander?' I asked. 'I'm not getting your name yet, but I will, very shortly. Can you do it again, can you give us that noise again? Move around the room? Come here, we're here in total respect to you —'

Danniella gasped and put her hands to her face. Footsteps were coming from another part of the room.

'D'you hear that?' I said. 'Please continue with your movements.'

We all looked towards the place where the sound had come from.

'Let us hear those footsteps again,' I said.

The sound came again. Danniella jumped and Angus cried, 'My goodness!' Alice smiled.

Now I knew the spirit was responding to my voice, I could ask him to come closer to us. He was out in the main body of the hall, while we were all standing in a group on the stage. 'Can you come forward to us?' I asked.

We waited. The noises continued, but they didn't come any closer.

'Alice, do you want to try and call out?' Danniella asked.

'I'm scared,' she whispered.

'Don't worry,' Danniella reassured her.

If the spirit man wasn't coming to us, I could go to him. 'I'm coming over!' I called.

I walked over to the area where the noises had come from and spoke aloud to all the spirits present, telling them that I could channel their energy and inviting them to step forward and express themselves.

Then I got a name: Purvis.

Alice nodded excitedly.

'When he mentioned the name "Purvis", I couldn't believe that. It's not a name he would have known.'

Alice

I felt Purvis come close to me. He had taken up the invitation.

Angus, Danniella and Alice all came down from the stage and drew close to me as they realized I was starting to channel the man.

'Who are you?' Angus asked.

'Purvis, Purv … is. I cannot do it, I cannot do it …' Purvis was bent over and speaking in a breathless whisper. 'I find it difficult to do this. I haven't done this.'

'I'd never seen channelling before. It scared me, but everyone assured me he was safe.'

Alice

'Was this your home? Was this where you were based?' asked Danniella.

'Yes, yes.'

'Is this where you died?' she continued.

'What happened to you?' Angus asked.

'It all went black, it all went black…'

'Are you having trouble breathing?' Danniella asked.

Everyone was concerned about the spirit. He had started to cough.

'The smoke, the smoke!'

Danniella turned to Alice. 'Did he crash?'

'Yes, there was a crash,' Alice said.

'A plane crash?'

Alice nodded.

'I don't know a lot about Purvis, but I do know that he crash-landed on this airfield and he unfortunately died. He's on the records, but that's really all I know. But that name really, really shook me, when Derek mentioned it.'

Alice

'Were you flying a plane at the time?' Danniella asked Purvis.

'Yes … Mayday, coming down, coming down…' Purvis sank down into a sitting position, head still bent. Angus caught hold of his shoulder to steady him.

'What was coming through was the spirit of a pilot falling to his death, burning...'

Angus

Then Purvis started shouting out a name over and over: 'Alan! Alan! Alan!' His voice echoed round the hall. 'He can't hear me!'

'That could have been his co-pilot,' said Angus.

'Could be,' Danniella agreed.

Alice felt confident enough to talk to Purvis now. 'This was a training base, wasn't it?' she said. 'Was it a happy place?'

'Very ... very ... happy.'

'I've seen lots of the photographs – there were lots of parties, lots of WAAFs.'

'The gin was good,' Purvis said.

Alice and Danniella smiled.

'D'you come here with your friends?' Angus asked.

'I do.'

'Do you dance?

'I certainly do. I do.'

Alice took up the questions again. 'Are you pleased with what we've done, with what we've restored?'

'Haven't finished.'

'We haven't finished yet, no.'

'We are waiting for you to finish.'

'Do you like people visiting here?' Angus asked, but at that moment Ray came in and brought me back. That was enough for now.

> **'It wasn't pleasant watching Derek channelling. He looked very uncomfortable. This spirit coming through him, it really took a lot of energy out of him.'**
>
> Angus

I found myself lying flat on my back in the hangar. What had happened?

'Hi, Derek,' Angus said. 'Just lie there and relax for a moment.'

'Would you like some water?' Danniella asked. She brought me some.

'We've just met someone who'd rather have a gin!' Angus told me.

While I rested for a moment to recover from the experience, Danniella asked Alice, 'Were you pleased with the result you got?'

'Yes,' she replied. 'I can't believe he came up with that name.'

That was the end of our investigation in Bedford, and of the first series too, but the Ghost Truck is still on the road, so watch out for us, we may be coming to your town. I hope to see you soon!

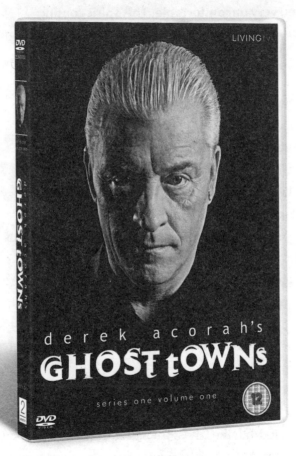